ULTIMATE MUSIC THEORY
GLORY ST. GERMAIN ARCT RMT.

Edited by Shelagh McKibbon-U'Ren RMT UMTC

PREP 1 RUDIMENTS

UltimateMusicTheory.com

ISBN: 978-0-9809556-6-8

ULTIMATE MUSIC THEORY: *The Way to Score Success!*

The Ultimate Music Theory workbooks are for all Musicians.

The more we understand the universal language of music, the more we are capable of communicating our ideas through performing and writing music, interpreting musical compositions of others, and developing a deeper appreciation of music. It is through music education that we progress from student to musician and are able to enjoy and understand music at a more comprehensive level.

Acknowledgements
Dedicated with love and gratitude to my husband Ray for his encouragement, and to our children Chrystal, Catherine, Ray Jr., David Joseph, Sherry Rose and our grandchildren, for their inspiration.

Respect Copyright

Published in 2011 by Gloryland Publishing
First printing - 2008.   Revised edition - 2011.
Third printing - 2018.
Printed in Canada.
GlorylandPublishing.com

UltimateMusicTheory.com

Library and Archives Canada Cataloguing in Publication St. Germain, Glory 1953-
Ultimate Music Theory Series / Glory St. Germain

Gloryland Publishing - Ultimate Music Theory Series:

GP - UP1	ISBN: 978-0-9809556-6-8	Ultimate Prep 1 Rudiments
GP - UP1A	ISBN: 978-0-9809556-9-9	Ultimate Prep 1 Rudiments Answer Book
GP - UP2	ISBN: 978-0-9809556-7-5	Ultimate Prep 2 Rudiments
GP - UP2A	ISBN: 978-0-9813101-0-7	Ultimate Prep 2 Rudiments Answer Book
GP- UBR	ISBN: 978-0-9813101-3-8	Ultimate Basic Rudiments
GP - UBRA	ISBN: 978-0-9813101-4-5	Ultimate Basic Answer Book
GP - UIR	ISBN: 978-0-9813101-5-2	Ultimate Intermediate Rudiments
GP - UIRA	ISBN: 978-0-9813101-6-9	Ultimate Intermediate Answer Book
GP - UAR	ISBN: 978-0-9813101-7-6	Ultimate Advanced Rudiments
GP - UARA	ISBN: 978-0-9813101-8-3	Ultimate Advanced Answer Book
GP - UCR	ISBN: 978-0-9813101-1-4	Ultimate Complete Rudiments
GP - UCRA	ISBN: 978-0-9813101-2-1	Ultimate Complete Answer Book

Ultimate Music Theory Prep 1 Rudiments
Table of Contents

Ultimate Music Theory - Prep 1 Guide & Chart

Score: **60 - 69** Pass; **70 - 79** Honors; **80 - 89** First Class Honors; **90 - 100** First Class Honors with Distinction

Ultimate Music Theory: *The Way to Score Success!*

ULTIMATE MUSIC THEORY: *The Way to Score Success!*

The focus of the **Ultimate Music Theory** Series is to simplify complex concepts and show the relativity of these concepts with practical application. These workbooks are designed to help teachers and students discover the excitement and benefits of a music theory education.

Ultimate Music Theory workbooks are based on a proven approach to the study of music theory that follows these **4 Ultimate Music Theory Learning Principles**:

♪ **Simplicity of Learning** - easy to understand instructions, examples and exercises.

♪ **Memory Joggers** - tips for all learning styles including auditory, visual and tactile.

♪ **Tie it All Together** - helping musicians understand the universal language of music.

♪ **Make it Relevant** - applying theoretical concepts to pedagogical studies.

The Ultimate Music Theory™ Rudiments Workbooks, Supplemental Workbooks and Exams help students prepare for successful completion of nationally recognized theory examinations including the Royal Conservatory of Music Theory Levels.

UMT Prep 1 Rudiments Workbook plus the PREP LEVEL Supplemental Workbook
= RCM Theory Preparatory Level (2016 Royal Conservatory of Music Theory Syllabus).

♫ Note: Additional completion of the LEVEL 1 Supplemental Workbook
= RCM Theory Level 1 (2016 Royal Conservatory of Music Theory Syllabus).

The Ultimate Music Theory Series includes these EXCLUSIVE BONUS features:

♪ **Ultimate Music Theory Guide & Chart** - convenient summarization to review concepts.

♪ **12 Comprehensive Review Tests** - support retention of concepts learned in previous lessons.

♫ **Note:** Each "♫ Note" points out important information and handy memory tips.

♪ **80 Ultimate Music Theory Flashcards** - Vocabulary, Musical Signs, Rhythm and More!
DOWNLOAD Your FREE Flashcards at UltimateMusicTheory.com FREE RESOURCES.

♫ **Note:** The convenient and easy to use Ultimate Music Theory Answer Books match the student workbooks for quick & accurate marking. Answer Books available for all levels.

♪ **Ultimate Music Theory FREE Resources - Instant access to Videos, Worksheets & Blog.**
Become a UMT MEMBER - Get Your FREE Flashcards, Lesson Plans, Certificate & More!

UltimateMusicTheory.com

Lesson 1   The Keyboard and the Musical Alphabet

The **KEYBOARD** consists of **WHITE** and **BLACK** keys. The black keys are found in groups of two and three. Each key has its own pitch (sound). When moving to the left on the keyboard, the pitch gets LOWER in sound. When moving to the right on the keyboard, the pitch gets HIGHER in sound.

The **BLACK** keys are found in groups of:

TWO   and   **THREE**

1. Circle the groups of two black keys going up the keyboard from the lowest to the highest.

LOWEST   HIGHEST

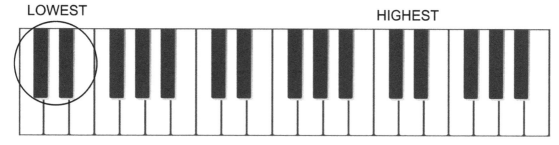

2. Circle the groups of three black keys going down the keyboard from the highest to the lowest.

LOWEST   HIGHEST

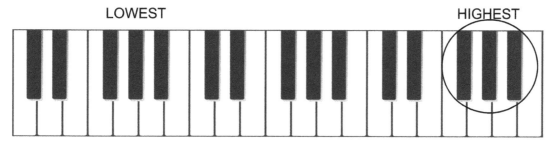

The **MUSICAL ALPHABET** consists of 7 letter names. The **WHITE** keys are **A B C D E F G**.

3. Copy the names of the white keys on the keyboard below.

A B C D E F G

F G A B C D E F G A B C D E

WHITE KEYS: C, D and E

C is the **WHITE** key on the left of the TWO black keys.

1. Name all the **C**'s directly on the keyboard. Circle the highest **C** directly on the keyboard.

D is the **WHITE** key in the middle of the TWO black keys.

2. Name all the **D**'s directly on the keyboard. Circle the highest **D** directly on the keyboard.

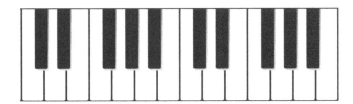

E is the **WHITE** key on the right of the TWO black keys.

3. Name all the **E**'s directly on the keyboard. Circle the highest **E** directly on the keyboard.

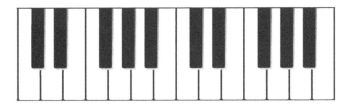

4. Name all the white keys **C**, **D** and **E** directly on the keyboard. Start from the lowest C, D, E (to the left on the keyboard) and continue up to the highest C, D, E (to the right on the keyboard).

WHITE KEYS: F, G, A and B

F is the **WHITE** key on the left of the THREE black keys.

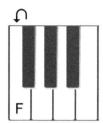

1. Name all the **F**'s directly on the keyboard.
   Circle the lowest **F** directly on the keyboard.

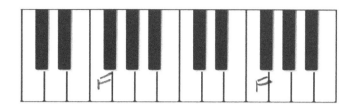

G is the **WHITE** key between the 1st and 2nd of the THREE black keys.

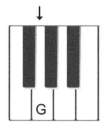

2. Name all the G's directly on the keyboard.
   Circle the lowest **G** directly on the keyboard.

A is the **WHITE** key between the 2nd and 3rd of the THREE black keys.

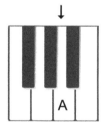

3. Name all the **A**'s directly on the keyboard.
   Circle the lowest **A** directly on the keyboard.

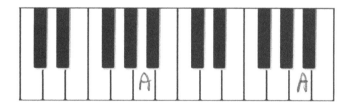

B is the **WHITE** key at the right of the THREE black keys.

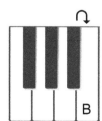

4. Name all the **B**'s directly on the keyboard.
   Circle the lowest **B** directly on the keyboard.

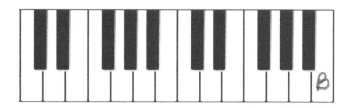

DRAWING the KEYBOARD and OCTAVES

DRAW a **KEYBOARD** by using the following steps:

Step 1: Draw a group of **TWO** popsicle sticks, then draw a group of **THREE** popsicle sticks.

1. Following the example, copy the group of two and the group of three popsicle sticks.

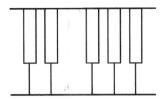 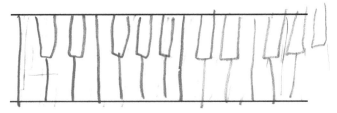

Step 2: Draw a line **in front** of the two popsicle sticks, **in between** the groups of two and three popsicle sticks, and **behind** (at the end of) the three popsicle sticks.

2. Following the example:
   a) Draw a group of two and a group of three popsicle sticks.
   b) Add lines in front, in between and behind the groups of popsicle sticks.

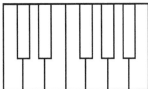 

When moving from one **KEY** to another **KEY** of the **SAME** name, the distance is **8 KEYS**. This is called an **OCTAVE**. When moving to the right, UP the keyboard, the sound gets higher in pitch. When moving to the left, DOWN the keyboard, the sound gets lower in pitch.

♫ **Note:** An octave is **8 keys** beginning and ending with the **SAME** letter name.

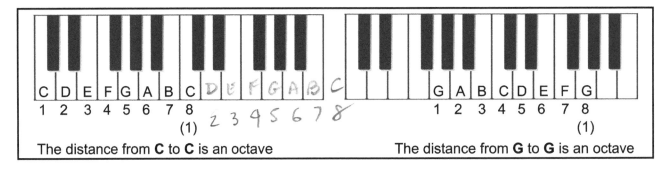

3. a) Name all the white keys within the octave from **C** to **C** directly on the keyboard.
   b) Write the numbers 1 - 8 below each letter name. This is called an _____.

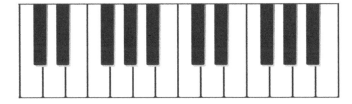

Lesson 1   Review Test

Total Score: ____

100

1. a) Circle **ALL** the groups of **TWO** black keys.
    b) Name all the **WHITE KEYS** within the octave from **D to D** directly on the keyboard.

10

2. a) Circle **ALL** the groups of **THREE** black keys.
    b) Name all the **WHITE KEYS** within the octave from **F to F** directly on the keyboard.

10

3. a) Circle the **HIGHEST BLACK KEY** on the **RIGHT** in each group of **THREE** black keys.
    b) Name all the **WHITE KEYS** within the octave from **A to A** directly on the keyboard.

10

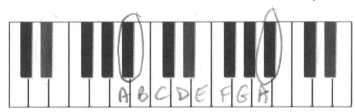

4. a) Circle the **LOWEST BLACK KEY** on the **LEFT** in each group of **TWO** black keys.
    b) Name all the **WHITE KEYS** within the octave from **C to C** directly on the keyboard.

10

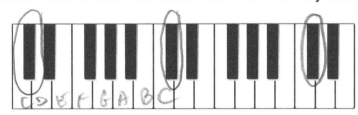

5. a) How many **octaves** from **C** to **C** are on the keyboard above? _____

    b) How many **groups** of **TWO** black keys are on the keyboard above? _____

10 c) How many **groups** of **THREE** black keys are on the keyboard above? _____

    d) How many **E**'s are on the keyboard above? _____

    e) How many **C**'s are on the keyboard above? _____

6. Name all the **WHITE KEYS** on the keyboard marked with a ☺.

10

C   G   B   C   F

7. Complete the **KEYBOARD** with groups of **TWO** and **THREE black keys**.

10

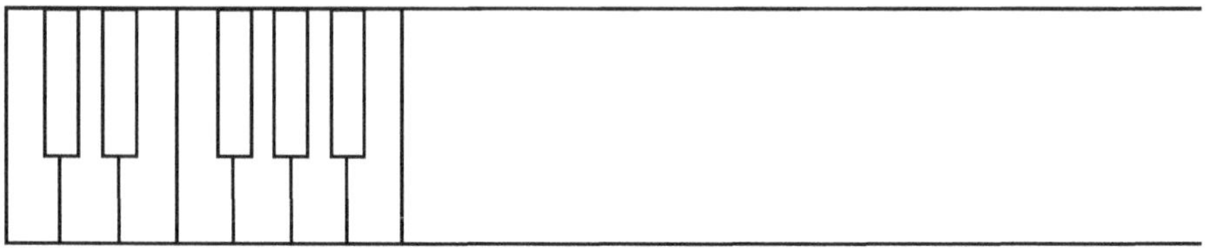

8. Name all the **WHITE KEYS** within the octave from **E** to **E** directly on the keyboard.

10

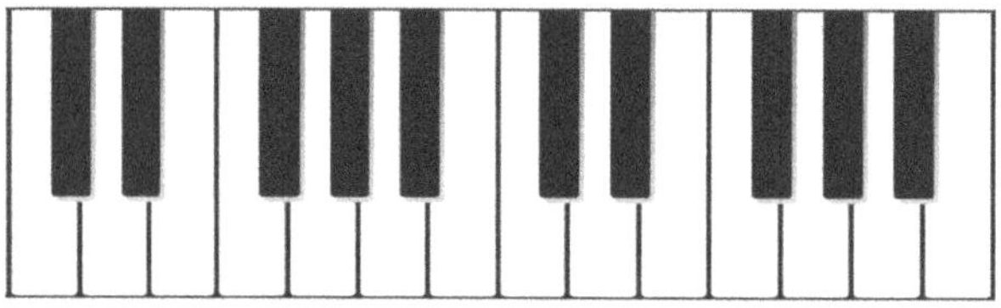

9. Name all the **WHITE KEYS** on the keyboard marked with a ☺.

10

—   —   —   —

10. a) What **word** do the letters on the keyboard above spell? _____

     b) How many times does the white key **"F"** appear on the keyboard above? _____

10 c) How many **octaves** of F to F are on the keyboard above? _____

     d) Write the **letter names** of the musical alphabet. _____

     e) How many letters are in the **musical alphabet**? _____

Lesson 2   The Staff - Treble Clef, Bass Clef, Landmarks and Notation

Music is written on a **STAFF**.

A **STAFF** consists of **FIVE lines** and **FOUR spaces**.

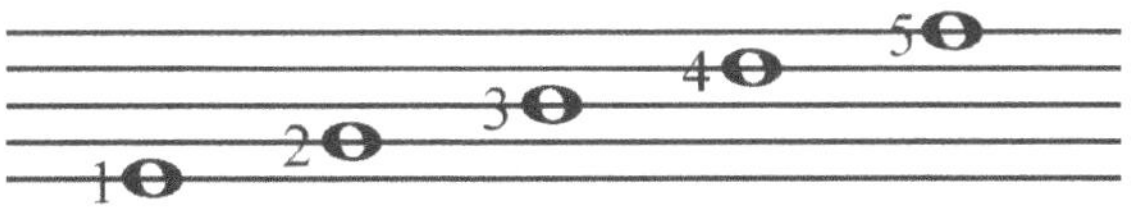

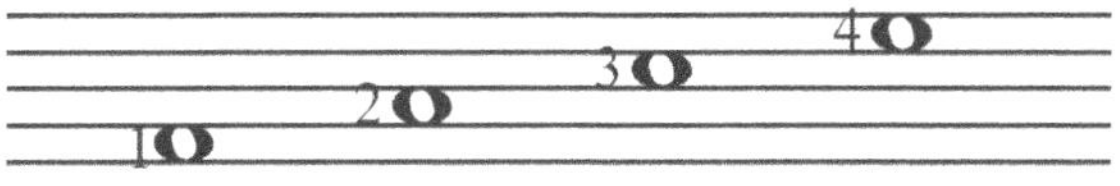

1. Number the 5 lines directly on the staff.

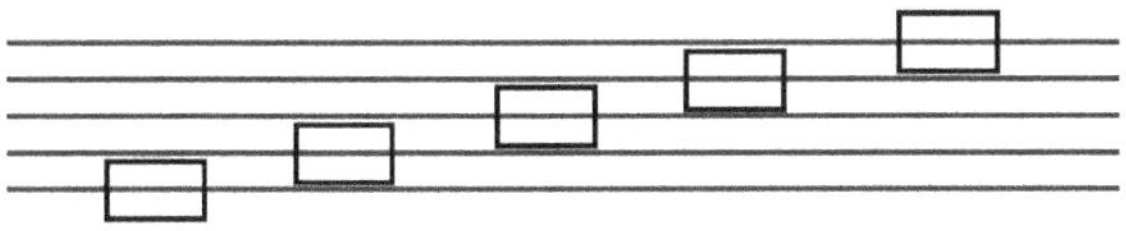

2. Number the 4 spaces directly on the staff.

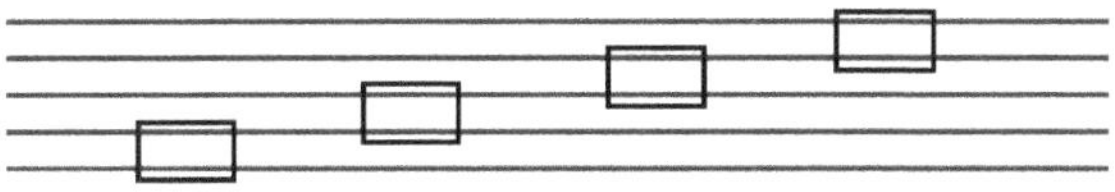

A **WHOLE NOTE** is written as a circle. ○

For a **LINE NOTE**, the line runs through the middle of the note.

For a **SPACE NOTE**, the note sits inside the space.

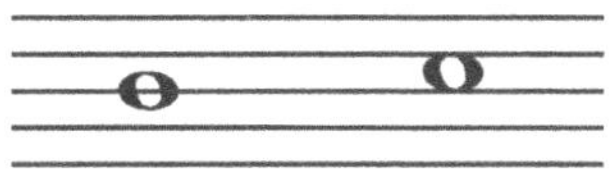

Line Note   Space Note

3. Draw a whole note on each of the 5 lines.

4. Identify the line number for each note.

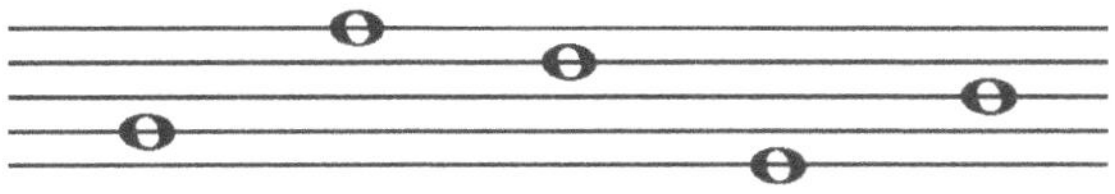

    2 ___ ___ ___ ___

5. Draw a whole note in each of the 4 spaces.

6. Identify the space number for each note.

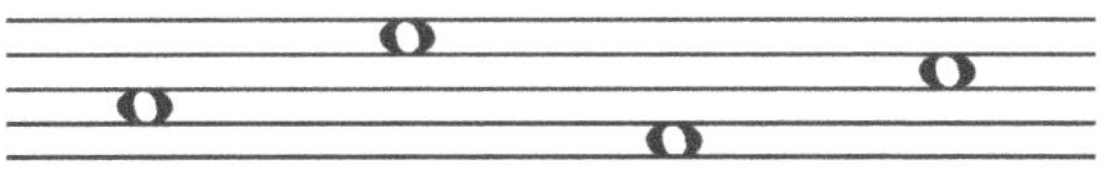

    2 ___ ___ ___

7. Draw a whole note on the following lines.

8. Draw a whole note in the following spaces.

Line   3   1   5   2   4   Space   4   2   3   1

DRAWING the TREBLE CLEF or G CLEF

CLEF signs are drawn at the beginning of the **STAFF**.

The **TREBLE CLEF** is also called the "**G**" Clef.

G line 2 →

1. Draw a Treble Clef on the staff by using the following steps:

Step 1: Begin **ABOVE** the staff and draw the letter "**J**" through the staff, ending in the space below the staff. This is the center line.

Step 2: Start at the top of the line and draw a "**P**" to line 4.

Step 3: Continue to draw a "**d**" from line 4 (semi-circle to the left) all the way to line 1.

Step 4: Continue to circle up to line 3 and curl around, finishing on line 2.

♫ **Note:** Line 2 is the "**G**" line in the **Treble Staff**. The lines used to draw the **Treble Clef** cross line 2, the "**G**" line, four times. This creates a **LANDMARK** for the note "**G**" in the **Treble Staff**.

Treble or G Clef	+	Staff	=	Treble Staff	Landmark note "G" in the Treble Staff
 		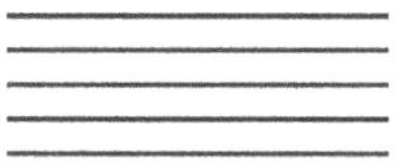			 

2. a) Draw Five Treble Clefs ("G" Clefs) on the staff below.
   b) Draw a whole note on the **G** line (line 2) after each Treble Clef.

DRAWING the BASS CLEF or F CLEF

DIFFERENT CLEF SIGNS are used to identify specific **PITCHES** on the keyboard.

The **BASS CLEF** is also called the "F" Clef.

F line 4 →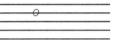

1. Draw a Bass Clef on the staff by using the following steps:

Step 1: Draw a black **DOT** on line 4. This is the "F" line.

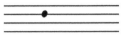 

Step 2: Draw **half of a heart**, curling up to line 5 of the staff and coming down to end in space 1.

 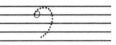

Step 3: Draw a **dot** in **SPACE 4** (above the "F" line) and a **dot** in **SPACE 3** (below the "F" line).

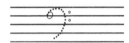

♫ **Note:** Line 4 is the "F" line in the **Bass Staff**. There is a dot **ON** line 4, **ABOVE** line 4 and **BELOW** line 4. This creates a **LANDMARK** for the note "F" in the **Bass Staff**.

Bass or F Clef	**+**	**Staff**	**=**	**Bass Staff**	**Landmark note "F" in the Bass Staff**

2. a) Draw Five Bass Clefs ("F" Clefs) on the staff below.
   b) Draw a whole note on the **F** line (line 4) after each Bass Clef.

LINE NOTES and SPACE NOTES in the TREBLE CLEF

The **Treble Clef** or **G Clef** curls around line 2.
This "**G**" line indicates the location of the white key **G** above Middle C on the keyboard.

♫ **Note:** When the Treble Clef is written on the staff it is called the Treble Staff or the Treble Clef.

Middle C and D are written **BELOW** the Treble Clef.

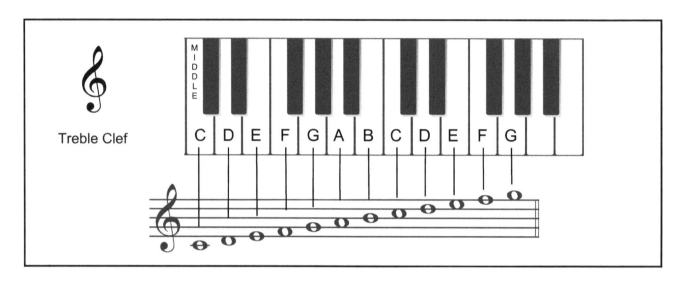

♫ **Note:** The Treble Clef **LINE NOTES** are: **E**very **G**ood **B**oy **D**eserves **F**un

1. Copy the line notes below. Use whole notes. Name the notes.

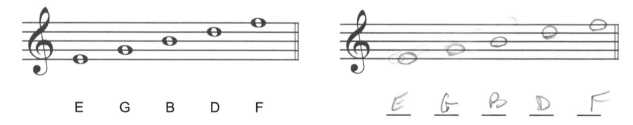

E   G   B   D   F   *E   G   B   D   F*

♫ **Note:** The Treble Clef **SPACE NOTES** are: **F A C E**   This spells **FACE**.

2. Copy the space notes below. Use whole notes. Name the notes.

F   A   C   E   *F   A   C   E*

MIDDLE C and D in the TREBLE CLEF

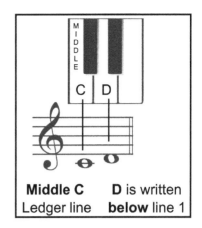

Middle **C** and **D** are written **BELOW** the **Treble Clef**.

Middle **C** is written on its own line called a **LEDGER line**.

♫ **Note:** Ledger lines must be **equal distance** from the
staff as they are extra staff lines used to extend
the staff as needed.

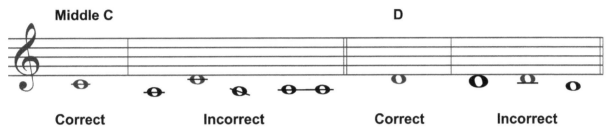

PITCH is how HIGH or LOW a note sounds. In music, the pitch moves high or low by movement from
one note to the next note. This movement creates a **PATTERN**.

When the **PATTERN** moves from one note to another note on the very **same line**, or from one note
to another note in the very **same space**, the note is **REPEATED** at the **same pitch**. This pattern is
called **SAME LINE** or **SAME SPACE**.

♫ **Note:** To write Middle C, draw the ledger line first and then draw the whole note for Middle C.
When drawing the ledger lines for Middle C, draw separate lines for each Middle C.
Do NOT join ledger lines.

1. Following the example, draw a Treble Clef and write three Middle C's below the Treble Clef.
   Use whole notes. The pattern created between each Middle C is "**SAME LINE**".

2. Following the example, draw a Treble Clef and write three D's below the Treble Clef.
   Use whole notes. The pattern created between each D is "**SAME SPACE**".

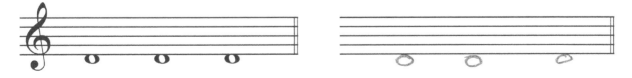

LINE NOTES in the TREBLE CLEF

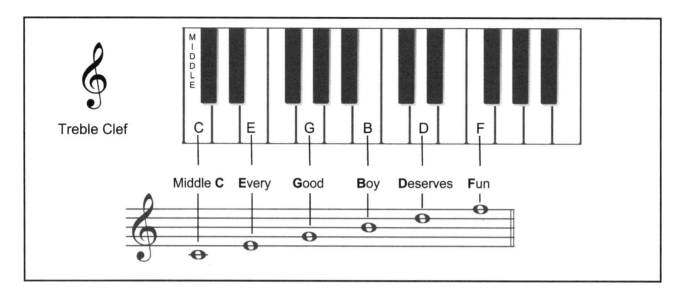

1. Name the following line notes in the Treble Clef.

_C_ _G_ _E_ _B_ _D_ _G_ _F_ _E_ _C_ _B_

2. Write the following line notes in the Treble Clef. Use whole notes.

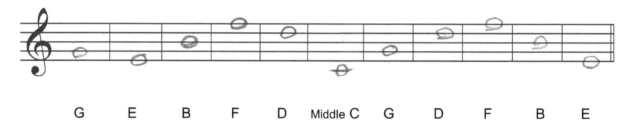

G   E   B   F   D   Middle C   G   D   F   B   E

3. Draw a Treble Clef at the beginning of the staff. Name the notes.

What words do they spell? _F_ _E_ _E_ _D_   _B_ _E_ _D_

LINE NOTES and SKIPS in the TREBLE CLEF

1. a) Name the following line notes in the Treble Clef.
   b) Draw a line from each note in the Treble Clef to the corresponding key on the keyboard (at the correct pitch).
   c) Name the key directly on the keyboard.

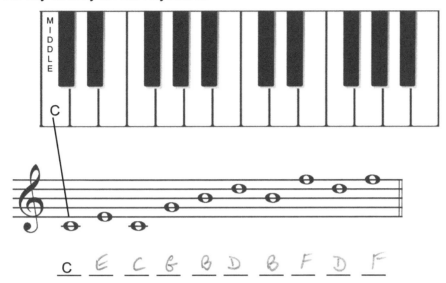

C E C G B D B F D F

2. Draw a Treble Clef at the beginning of the staff. Write the following line notes. Use whole notes.

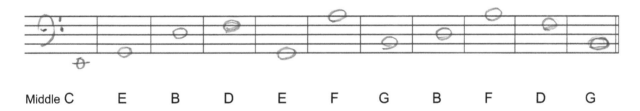

Middle C   E   B   D   E   F   G   B   F   D   G

In music, when moving from one LINE note to the next LINE note (skipping a space) or from one SPACE note to the next SPACE note (skipping a line), the pattern is called a **SKIP**.

A **SKIP** will also have direction. When a SKIP moves UP (getting higher in pitch), it is called **SKIP UP**. When a SKIP moves DOWN (getting lower in pitch), it is called **SKIP DOWN**.

♫ **Note:** A **Skip** moves from **LINE** to **LINE** (skipping a space) or **SPACE** to **SPACE** (skipping a line).

3. Copy the patterns below. Use whole notes. Name the notes.

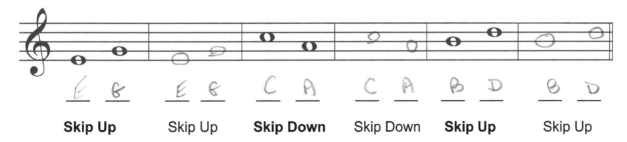

E G   E G   C A   C A   B D   B D

Skip Up   Skip Up   **Skip Down**   Skip Down   **Skip Up**   Skip Up

SPACE NOTES in the TREBLE CLEF

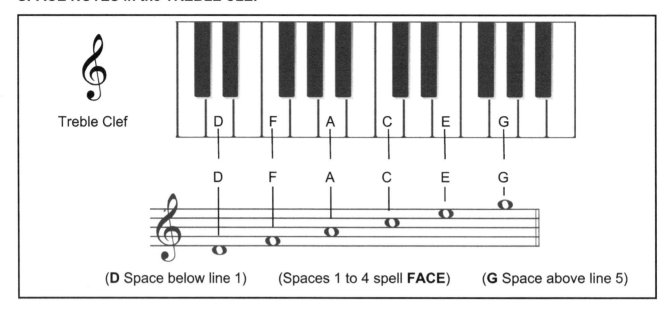

Treble Clef

(**D** Space below line 1)   (Spaces 1 to 4 spell **FACE**)   (**G** Space above line 5)

1. Name the following space notes in the Treble Clef.

F   D   C   A   E   G   F   C   D   E

2. Write the following space notes in the Treble Clef. Use whole notes.

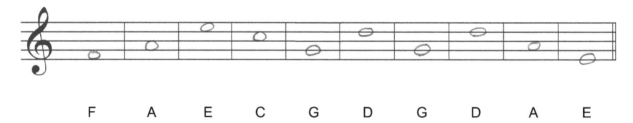

F   A   E   C   G   D   G   D   A   E

3. Draw a Treble Clef at the beginning of the staff. Name the notes.

What words do they spell? D   A   D   F   A   C   E   G   E   E

SPACE NOTES and STEPS in the TREBLE CLEF

1. a) Name the following space notes in the Treble Clef.
    b) Draw a line from each note in the Treble Clef to the corresponding key on the keyboard
       (at the correct pitch).
    c) Name the key directly on the keyboard.

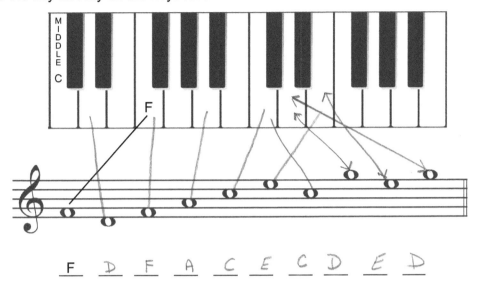

<u>F</u>   <u>D</u>   <u>F</u>   <u>A</u>   <u>C</u>   <u>E</u>   <u>C</u>   <u>D</u>   <u>E</u>   <u>D</u>

2. Draw a Treble Clef at the beginning of the staff. Write the following space notes.
    Use whole notes.

    D   C   E   F   A   G   F   G   A   C   D   E

In music, when moving from one LINE note to the next SPACE note, or from one SPACE note to the next LINE note, the pattern is called a **STEP**.

A **STEP** will also have direction. When a STEP moves UP (getting higher in pitch), it is called **STEP UP**. When a STEP moves DOWN (getting lower in pitch), it is called **STEP DOWN**.

♫ **Note:** A **STEP** moves from a **LINE** to the next **SPACE** or a **SPACE** to the next **LINE**.

3. Copy the patterns below. Use whole notes. Name the notes.

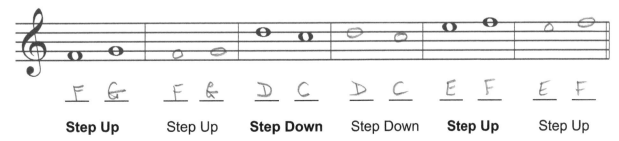

   <u>F</u> <u>G</u>   <u>F</u> <u>G</u>   <u>D</u> <u>C</u>   <u>D</u> <u>C</u>   <u>E</u> <u>F</u>   <u>E</u> <u>F</u>

   Step Up   Step Up   **Step Down**   Step Down   **Step Up**   Step Up

LINE NOTES and SPACE NOTES in the BASS CLEF

The **Bass Clef** or **F Clef** has 2 dots. One dot goes in the space **ABOVE** line 4 and the other dot goes in the space **BELOW** line 4. This "F" line indicates the location of the white key **F** below Middle C on the keyboard.

♫ **Note:** When the Bass Clef is written on the staff it is called the Bass Staff or the Bass Clef.

Middle C and B are written **ABOVE** the Bass Clef.

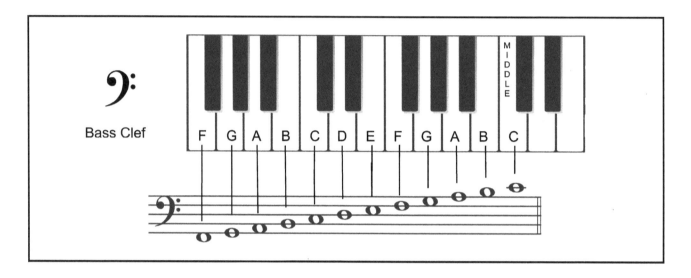

♫ **Note:** The Bass Clef **LINE NOTES** are: **G**ood **B**oys **D**eserve **F**un **A**lways

1. Copy the line notes below. Use whole notes. Name the notes.

G   B   D   F   A   G   B   D   F   A

♫ **Note:** The Bass Clef **SPACE NOTES** are: **A**ll **C**ows **E**at **G**rass

2. Copy the space notes below. Use whole notes. Name the notes.

A   C   E   G   A   C   E   G

B and MIDDLE C in the BASS CLEF

B and **Middle C** are written **ABOVE** the **Bass Clef**.

Middle C is written on its own line called a **LEDGER line**.

♫ **Note:** Ledger lines are written **slightly longer** than the note written on them. A separate ledger line is used for each note.

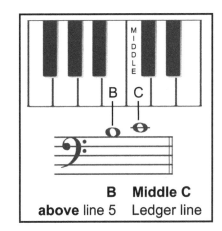

PITCH is how HIGH or LOW a note sounds. Sounds can get higher in pitch (ascend), get lower in pitch (descend) or stay at the same pitch. Movement between notes creates a **PATTERN**.

When the **PATTERN** moves from one note to another note on the very **same line**, or from one note to another note in the very **same space**, the note is **REPEATED** at the same pitch. This pattern is called **SAME LINE** or **SAME SPACE**.

♫ **Note:** To write Middle C, draw the ledger line first and then draw the whole note for Middle C. When drawing the ledger lines for Middle C, draw separate lines for each Middle C. Do NOT join ledger lines.

1. Following the example, draw a Bass Clef and write three Middle C's above the Bass Clef. Use whole notes. The pattern created between each Middle C is "**SAME LINE**".

2. Following the example, draw a Bass Clef and write three B's above the Bass Clef. Use whole notes. The pattern created between each B is "**SAME SPACE**".

LINE NOTES in the BASS CLEF

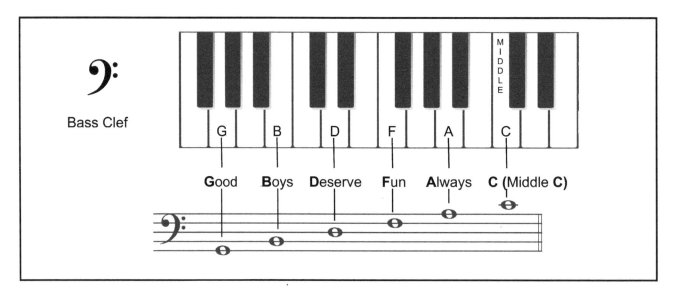

Bass Clef

Good Boys Deserve Fun Always C (Middle C)

1. Name the following line notes in the Bass Clef.

G D B A F C(Middle) D G F C(middle)

2. Write the following line notes in the Bass Clef. Use whole notes.

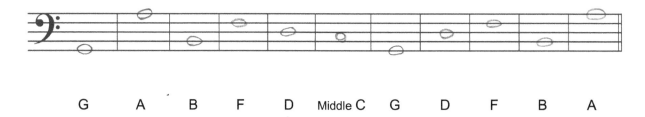

G   A   B   F   D   Middle C   G   D   F   B   A

3. Draw a Bass Clef at the beginning of the staff. Name the notes.

What words do they spell?   B A G   C A B

LINE NOTES and SKIPS in the BASS CLEF

1. a) Name the following line notes in the Bass Clef.
    b) Draw a line from each note in the Bass Clef to the corresponding key on the keyboard
       (at the correct pitch).
    c) Name the key directly on the keyboard.

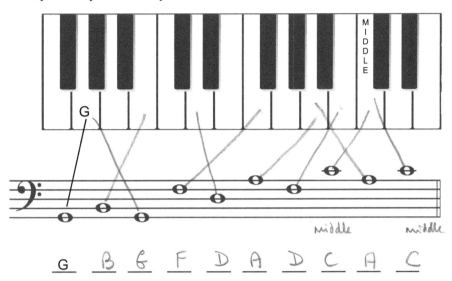

G   B   G   F   D   A   D   C   A   C

2. Draw a Bass Clef at the beginning of the staff. Write the following line notes. Use whole notes.

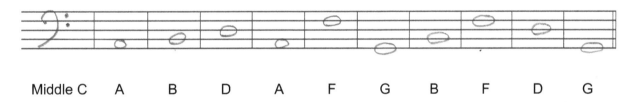

Middle C   A   B   D   A   F   G   B   F   D   G

3. Fill in the blanks:

    a) The pattern moving from one line to the next line is called a ___skip___.

    b) When a note moves from a line to a line, it will skip a ___note___.

4. Name the notes. Circle the correct pattern below.

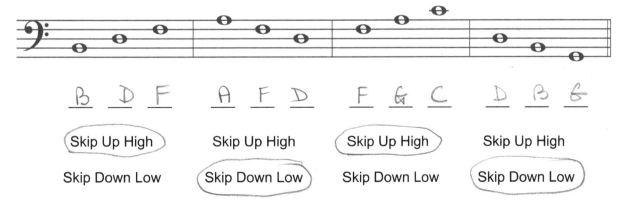

B   D   F   A   F   D   F   G   C   D   B   G

(Skip Up High)   Skip Up High   (Skip Up High)   Skip Up High

Skip Down Low   (Skip Down Low)   Skip Down Low   (Skip Down Low)

SPACE NOTES in the BASS CLEF

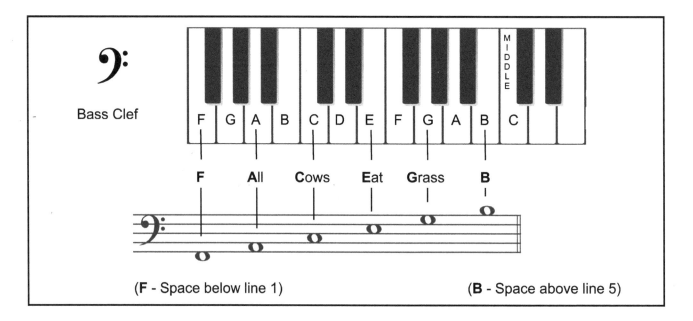

(**F** - Space below line 1)   (**B** - Space above line 5)

1. Name the following space notes in the Bass Clef.

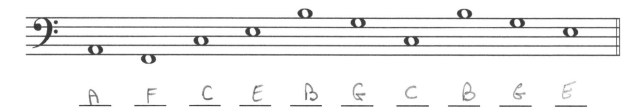

A   F   C   E   B   G   C   B   G   E

2. Write the following space notes in the Bass Clef. Use whole notes.

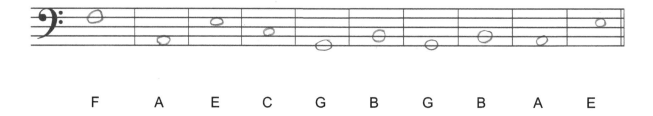

F   A   E   C   G   B   G   B   A   E

3. Draw a Bass Clef at the beginning of the staff. Name the notes.

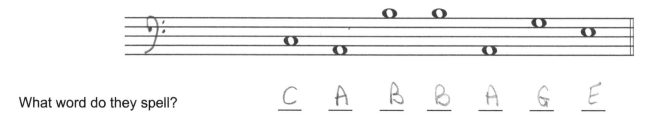

What word do they spell?   C   A   B   B   A   G   E

SPACE NOTES and STEPS in the BASS CLEF

1. a) Name the following space notes.
   b) Draw a line from each note in the Bass Clef to the corresponding key on the keyboard (at the correct pitch).
   c) Name the key directly on the keyboard.

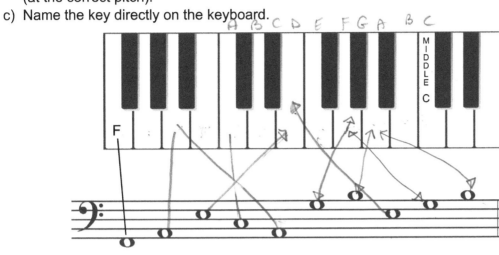

F   A   E   C   A   G   A   E   G   A

2. Draw a Bass Clef at the beginning of the staff. Write the following space notes. Use whole notes.

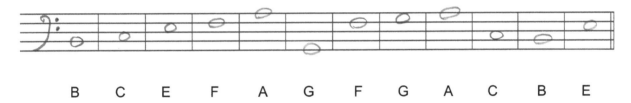

B   C   E   F   A   G   F   G   A   C   B   E

3. Fill in the blanks:

   a) The PATTERN moving from one LINE to the next SPACE is called a ___step___ .

   b) The PATTERN moving from one SPACE to the next LINE is called a ___step___ .

4. Name the notes. Circle the correct pattern below.

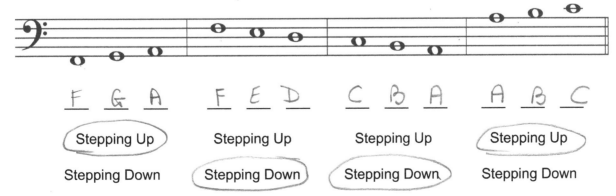

F   G   A   F   E   D   C   B   A   A   B   C

(Stepping Up)   Stepping Up   Stepping Up   (Stepping Up)

Stepping Down   (Stepping Down)   (Stepping Down)   Stepping Down

Lesson 2   Review Test

Total Score: ____
/ 100

1. Draw a **Treble Clef** at the beginning of the staff. Name the notes.

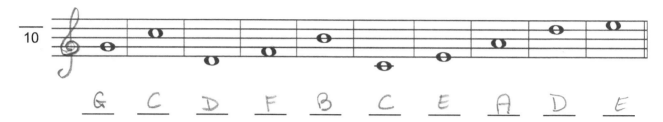

G   C   D   F   B   C   E   A   D   E

2. Draw a **Bass Clef** at the beginning of the staff. Name the notes.

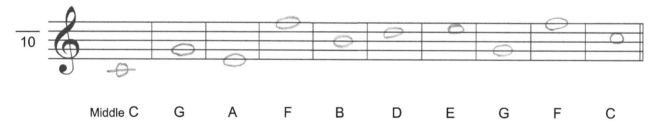

F   A   C   E   C   B   D   G   B   A

3. Write the following notes in the **Treble Clef**. Use whole notes.

Middle C   G   A   F   B   D   E   G   F   C

4. Write the following notes in the **Bass Clef**. Use whole notes.

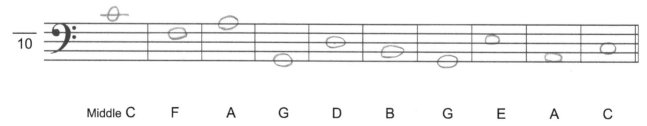

Middle C   F   A   G   D   B   G   E   A   C

5. a) Complete the **KEYBOARD** with groups of **TWO** and **THREE** black keys.
b) Write the name of each **WHITE** key directly on the keyboard below.

10

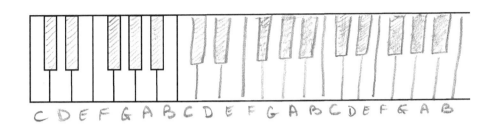

6. Name the following notes in the **Treble Clef**. Circle the correct pattern below.

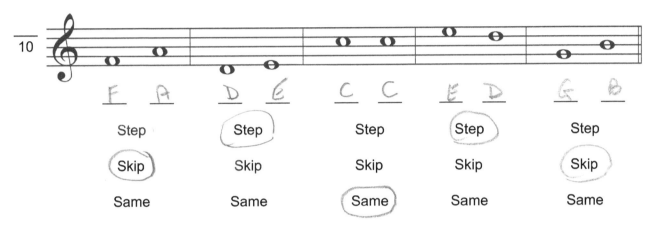

7. Name the following notes in the **Bass Clef**. Circle the correct pattern below.

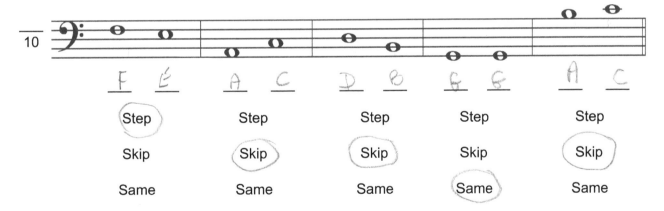

8. Draw a **Treble Clef** at the beginning of the staff. Write the following **SPACE** notes. Use whole notes.

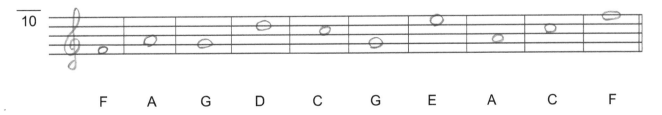

| F | A | G | D | C | G | E | A | C | F |

9. Draw a **Bass Clef** at the beginning of the staff. Write the following **LINE** notes. Use whole notes.

10

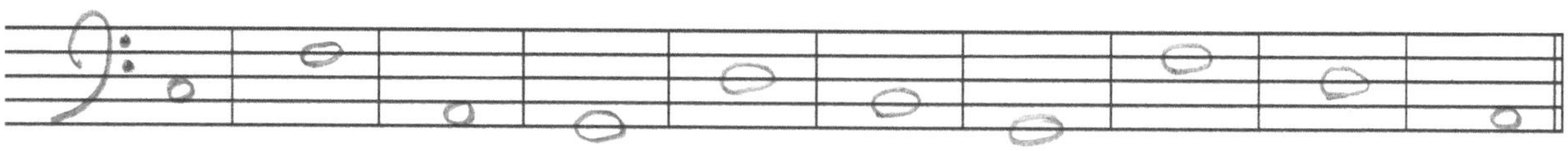

Middle C   F   A   G   D   B   G   F   D   A

10. Match each musical term with the English definition. (Not all definitions will be used.)

10

Term		Definition
step	f	a) F Clef
Treble Clef	c	b) short line used for Middle C
octave	g	c) G Clef
ledger line	b	d) groups of 2 and 3
black keys	d	e) five
musical alphabet	h	f) line note to space note or space note to line note
Bass Clef	a	g) 8 keys beginning and ending with the same letter name
number of lines on the staff	e	h) A B C D E F G
number of spaces on the staff	k	i) line note to line note or space note to space note
skip	i	j) ten
		k) four

Lesson 3   Patterns and the Grand Staff

In music, the movement from one note to the next note creates a **PATTERN**.
The **PITCH** (high or low sound) will vary depending upon the direction of the pattern.

When moving from one line note to the same
line note, the pattern is called **SAME LINE**.

When moving from one space note to the same
space note, the pattern is called **SAME SPACE**.

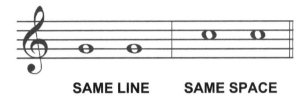

SAME LINE   **SAME SPACE**

When stepping from one line note to the next space
note, or from one space note to the next line note,
the pattern is called **STEP UP** or **STEP DOWN**.

STEP UP   **STEP DOWN**

When skipping from one line note to the next line
note (skipping a space), or from one space note to
the next space note (skipping a line), the pattern
is called **SKIP UP** or **SKIP DOWN**.

SKIP UP   **SKIP DOWN**

1. Identify the patterns between each pair of notes as:
   same line, same space, step up, step down, skip up or skip down.

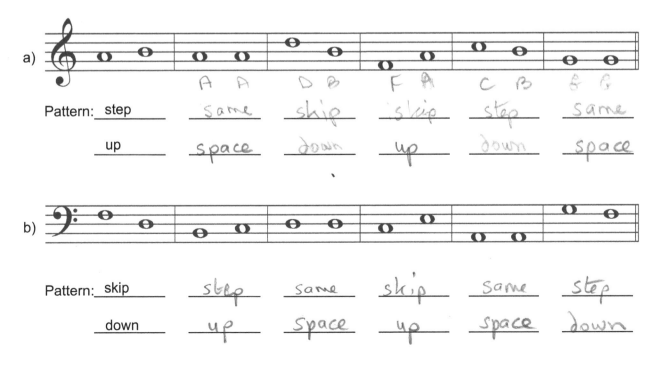

a)

Pattern: _step_ _Same_ _skip_ _skip_ _step_ _same_
_up_ _space_ _down_ _up_ _down_ _space_

b)

Pattern: _skip_ _step_ _same_ _skip_ _same_ _step_
down _up_ _space_ _up_ _space_ _down_

IDENTIFYING PATTERNS

When **IDENTIFYING** the **PATTERN**, identify the direction first (up, down or same). Then identify the distance (step, skip, same line or same space).

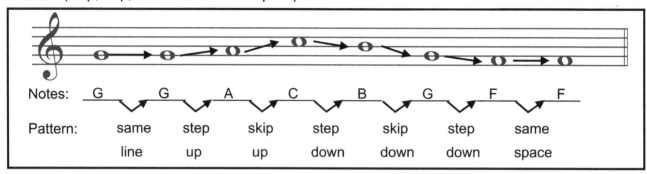

Notes:	G	G	A	C	B	G	F	F
Pattern:		same line	step up	skip up	step down	skip down	step down	same space

1. Identify the pattern between each pair of notes in the Treble Clef as:
   same line, same space, step up, step down, skip up or skip down. Name the notes.

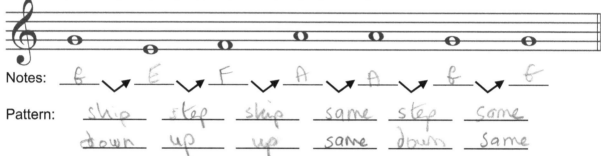

Notes:	G	E	F	A	A	G	G
Pattern:	skip down	step up	skip up	same same	step down	same same	

2. Identify the pattern between each pair of notes in the Bass Clef as:
   same line, same space, step up, step down, skip up or skip down. Name the notes.

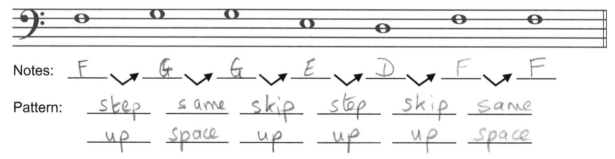

Notes:	F	G	G	E	D	F	F
Pattern:	step up	same space	skip up	step up	skip up	same space	

3. Fill in the blanks:

a) When a note is REPEATED at the SAME PITCH:
   A LINE NOTE will go to a note on the SAME ___space___.
   A SPACE NOTE will go to a note in the SAME ___space___.

b) When stepping from one note to the very next note:
   A LINE NOTE will step to a ___space___ note.
   A SPACE NOTE will step to a ___line___ note.

c) When skipping from one note to another note (skipping over a note):
   A LINE NOTE will skip to a ___line___ note (skipping a ___space note___)
   A SPACE NOTE will skip to a ___space___ note (skipping a ___line note___)

THE GRAND STAFF

The **GRAND STAFF** is made up of the Treble Clef and Bass Clef joined together by a **BRACE** or **BRACKET** and a **bar line**.

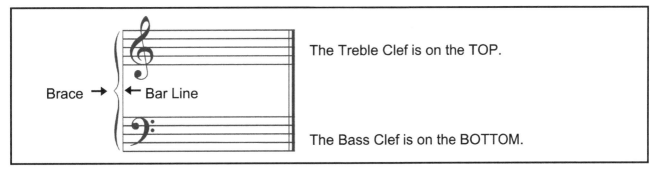

The Treble Clef is on the TOP.

Brace → ← Bar Line

The Bass Clef is on the BOTTOM.

1. Draw a brace in front of the Grand Staff by using the following steps:

Step 1: Draw a bar line from the top of the Treble Clef to the bottom of the Bass Clef **before drawing the brace**.

Step 2: Draw a curved line from the top of the Treble Clef to the middle of the Grand Staff.

Step 3: Draw a "sideways v" at the bottom of the curved line.

Step 4: Draw another curved line from the bottom of the "sideways v" to the bottom of the Bass Clef.

2. a) Trace the brace on the first Grand Staff.
   b) Draw a brace to complete each Grand Staff below.

BAR LINES and MEASURES

BAR LINES are lines that divide the music into equal **MEASURES** of time.

In the Grand Staff, the BAR LINE is written from the TOP of the Grand staff (line 5 of the Treble Staff) to the BOTTOM of the Grand Staff (line 1 of the Bass Staff).

There are three types of **BAR LINES**:

1. A bar line (a single thin line) divides the music into equal measures of time.
2. A double bar line (two thin bar lines together) indicates the end of a section.
3. A double bar line (a thin bar line and a thick bar line together) indicates the end of the music.

A double bar line is often referred to as a final bar line when used at the end of a piece of music.

One way of indicating **MEASURE NUMBERS** is by writing the number inside a small box above the top left of each MEASURE.

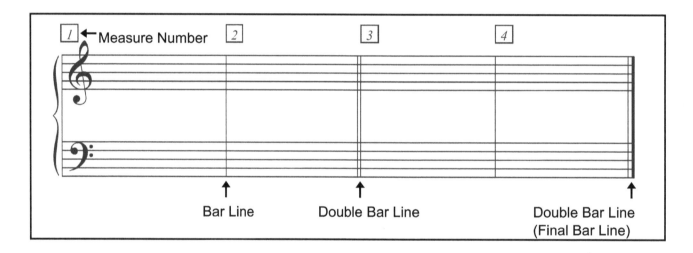

1. a) Draw a brace at the beginning of the Grand Staff.
   b) Divide the Grand Staff into **4** equal measures.
   c) Number each measure inside the measure box at the beginning of each measure.
   d) Draw a double bar line at the end of the second measure and a double bar line (final bar line) at the end of the Grand Staff.

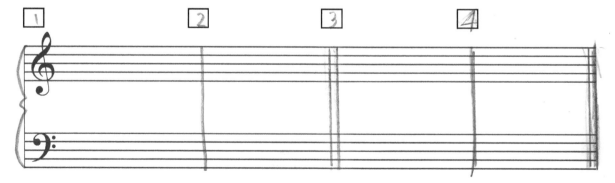

PITCHES on the KEYBOARD

NOTES written on the **GRAND STAFF** correspond to specific **PITCHES** on the keyboard.

The lower the note on the Grand Staff (to the left on the keyboard), the lower the pitch.
As notes move up the Grand Staff (to the right on the keyboard), the sound gets higher in pitch.

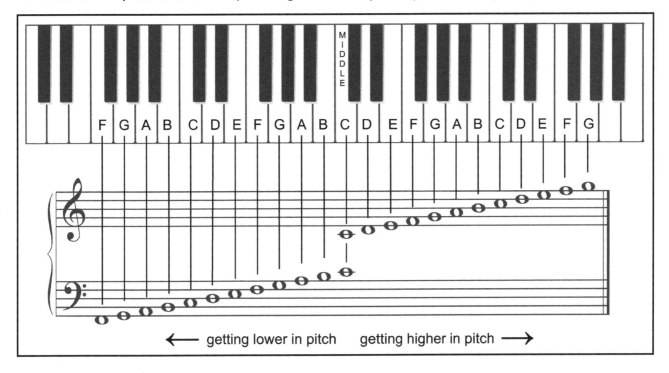

← getting lower in pitch   getting higher in pitch →

1. a) Name the following notes on the Grand Staff.
   b) Draw a line from each note to the corresponding key on the keyboard (at the correct pitch).
   c) Name the key directly on the keyboard.

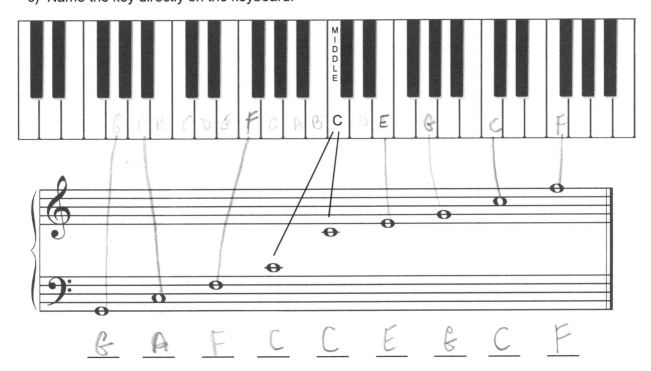

G   A   F   C   C   E   G   C   F

"G B D F" PATTERNS on the GRAND STAFF

LANDMARK NOTES are used to quickly identify notes on the Grand Staff. They are defined by their PITCH and by their PLACEMENT ON THE GRAND STAFF.

The Landmark Skipping Pattern of "**G B D F**" can be found 3 times on the Grand Staff:

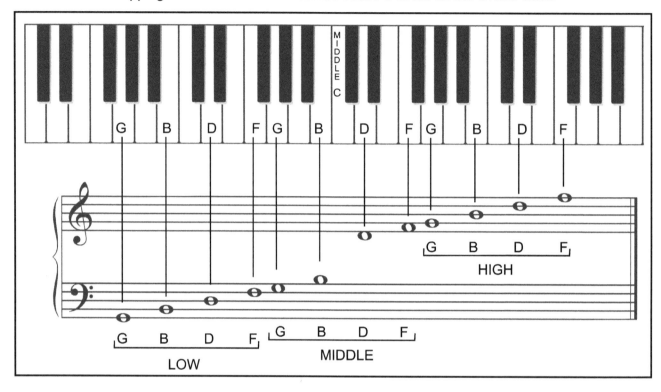

1. a) Name the following notes on the Grand Staff.
   b) Draw a line from each note to the corresponding key on the keyboard (at the correct pitch).
   c) Name the key directly on the keyboard.

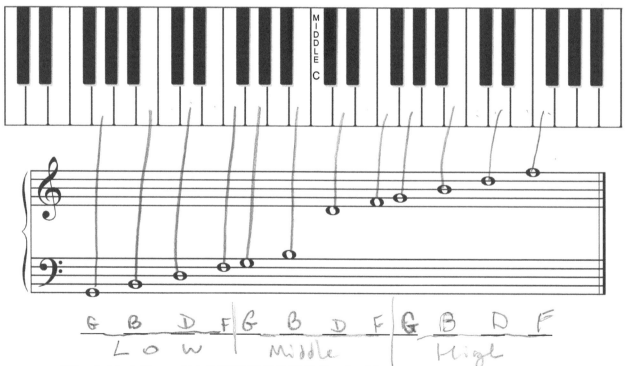

34

"A C E" PATTERNS on the GRAND STAFF

The Landmark Skipping Pattern of "**A C E**" can be found 3 times on the Grand Staff.

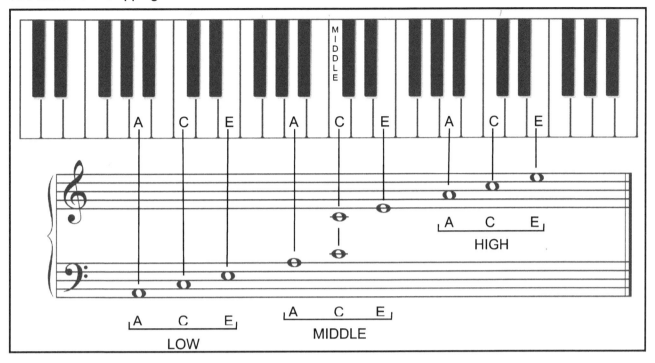

♫ **Note:** When the Middle C is written closer to the Bass Clef, it is part of the Bass Clef. When the Middle C is written closer to the Treble Clef, it is part of the Treble Clef. Both the Bass Clef Middle C and the Treble Clef Middle C are the **SAME Middle C** on the keyboard.

1. a) Name the following notes on the Grand Staff.
   b) Draw a line from each note to the corresponding key on the keyboard (at the correct pitch).
   c) Name the key directly on the keyboard.

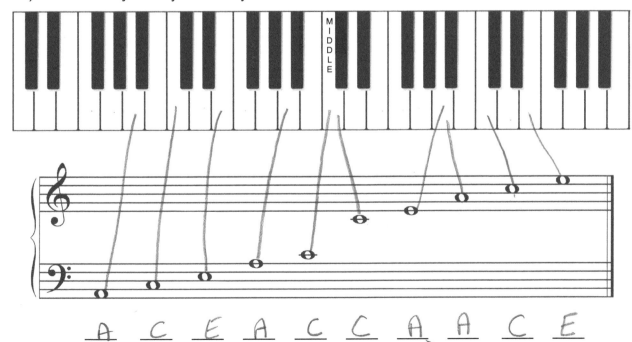

A   C   E   A   C   C   A   A   C   E

Lesson 3   Review Test

Total Score: ____
100

1. Draw a **Bass Clef** at the beginning of the staff. Name the notes.

10

G D A G C B F C A E

2. Write the following notes in the **Treble Clef**. Use whole notes.

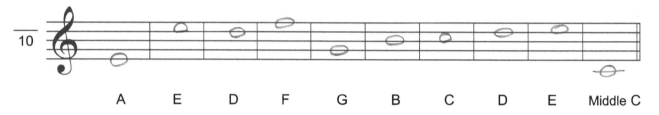

10

A   E   D   F   G   B   C   D   E   Middle C

3. a) Circle **ALL** the groups of **TWO black** keys.
   b) Write the names of the white keys **C**, **D** and **E** directly on the keyboard below.

10

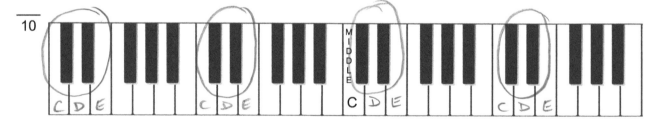

4. a) Draw a **brace** at the beginning of the Grand Staff.
   b) Divide the Grand Staff into **4** measures.
   c) Number each measure inside the measure box at the beginning of each measure.
   10 d) Draw a **double bar line** (final bar line) at the end.

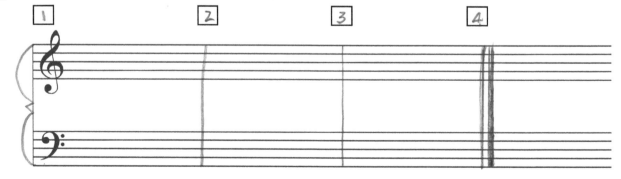

5. Identify the **PATTERN** between each pair of notes in the **Treble Clef** as:
same line, same space, step up, step down, skip up or skip down. Name the notes.

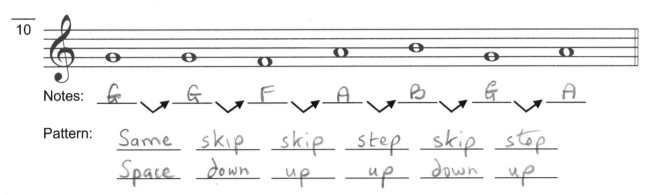

Notes: G   G   F   A   B   G   A

Pattern:
Same   skip   skip   step   skip   step
Space   down   up   up   down   up

6. Identify the **PATTERN** between each pair of notes in the **Bass Clef** as:
same line, same space, step up, step down, skip up or skip down. Name the notes.

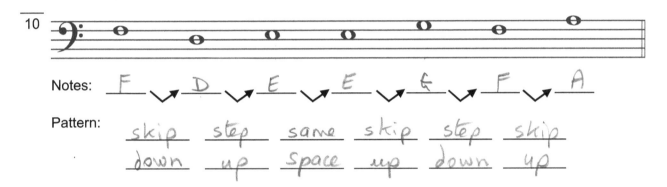

Notes: F   D   E   E   G   F   A

Pattern:
skip   step   same   skip   step   skip
down   up   Space   up   down   up

7. a) Name the following notes on the Grand Staff.
b) Draw a line from each note to the corresponding key on the keyboard (at the correct pitch).
c) Name the key directly on the keyboard.

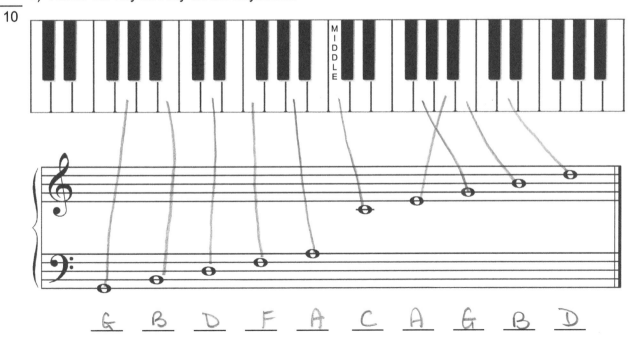

G   B   D   F   A   C   A   G   B   D

8. Add a **BRACE** to the Grand Staff. Name the notes.

10

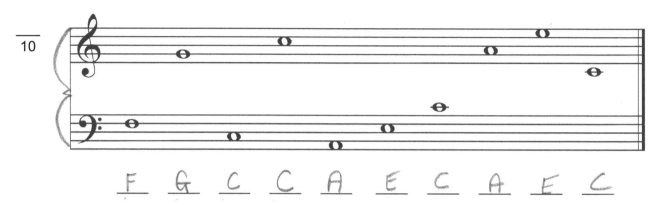

F   G   C   C   A   E   C   A   E   C

9. Draw a **Bass Clef** at the beginning of the staff. Write the following **LINE** notes.
Use whole notes.

10

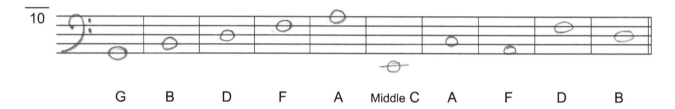

G   B   D   F   A   Middle C   A   F   D   B

10. Match each musical term with the English definition. (Not all definitions will be used.)

10

Term		Definition
pitch	b	a) line note to the same line note
skipping a line	e	b) sound (high or low)
brace	g	c) short line used for Middle C
step	k	d) space note to the next space note
musical alphabet	j	e) line note to the next line note
ledger line	c	f) space note to the same space note
same line	a	g) bracket that joins the Treble Clef and
same space	f	the Bass Clef to form the Grand Staff
skipping a space	d	h) bottom of the 3 black keys
Grand Staff	i	i) Treble Clef and Bass Clef joined together
		j) A B C D E F G
		k) line note to the next space note or
		space note to the next line note

Lesson 4   Note and Rest Values

A **NOTE** symbolizes **SOUND** in music. The placement of the **NOTEHEAD** on the staff indicates the pitch (high or low). The notehead fills one space or has one line running through it.

STEMS, **DOTS**, **FLAGS** and **BEAMS** are used to indicate duration (long or short) of sound.

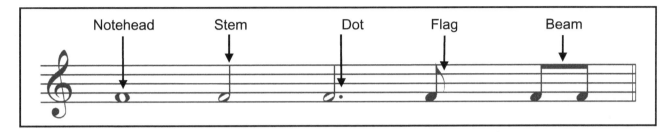

Each **NOTE** has a specific time value.

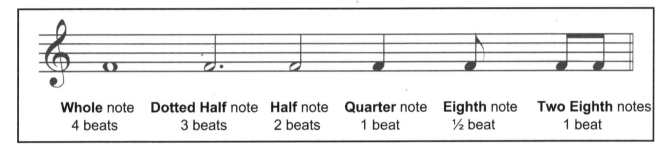

Whole note	Dotted Half note	Half note	Quarter note	Eighth note	Two Eighth notes
4 beats	3 beats	2 beats	1 beat	½ beat	1 beat

1. Write the number of beats each note receives.

Beats: 4   3   2   1   ½   1

2. Complete the following Note Value Chart:

One whole note equals __2__ half notes	𝅝 4	=	𝅗𝅥 2 𝅗𝅥 2
Two half notes equal __4__ quarter notes	𝅗𝅥 2 𝅗𝅥 2	=	♩ ♩ ♩ ♩
Four quarter notes equal __8__ eighth notes	♩ ♩ ♩ ♩	=	♫ ♫ ♫ ♫

NOTE VALUES

A **WHOLE** note is written as a circle. It fills a space as a **SPACE** note, or has a line running through the middle as a **LINE** note.

1. Write three whole notes in space 1 and three whole notes on line 3.
   A whole note receives ____4____ beats.

A **HALF** note is written as a circle with a stem. To identify the direction of the stem, follow the **Stem Rules**.

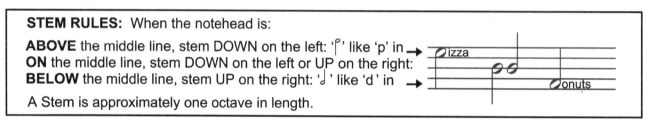

STEM RULES: When the notehead is:

ABOVE the middle line, stem DOWN on the left: 'ꟼ' like 'p' in → ꟼizza
ON the middle line, stem DOWN on the left or UP on the right:
BELOW the middle line, stem UP on the right: 'd' like 'd' in → donuts

A Stem is approximately one octave in length.

2. Copy the following half notes. The stem may go up or down for notes written on line 3.
   A half note receives ____2____ beats.

A **DOTTED HALF** note is written as a half note with a **dot**. To identify the placement of the dot, follow the **Dot Placement Rules**.

DOT PLACEMENT RULES:
For **SPACE** notes: dot placed in the space to the right of the notehead. →
For **LINE** notes: dot placed above the line, in the space to the right →
of the notehead. **Never write a dot directly on a line.**

3. Copy the following dotted half notes. A dotted half note receives ____3____ beats.

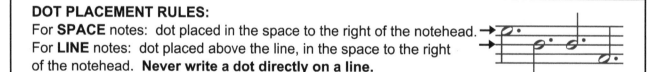

A **QUARTER** note is a black notehead with a stem.

4. Copy the following quarter notes. A quarter note receives ____1____ beat.

An **EIGHTH** note is written as a quarter note with a flag. Follow the Stem Rules.
The flag **ALWAYS** goes to the right. The end of the flag does **NOT** touch the notehead.

5. Copy the following eighth notes. An eighth note receives _____ beat.

Two **EIGHTH** notes may be joined together with a **BEAM**. Together, they receive **ONE** beat.

BEAM RULES:
The notehead **furthest away from the middle line** determines
the stem direction. If both notes are the same distance, the
stems can go up or down. The beam joins the 2 eighth notes
at the end of the stems.

6. Copy the following beamed eighth notes. Two beamed eighth notes receive _____ beat.

7. Add stems to the following noteheads to create quarter notes. Follow the Stem Rules.

8. Add flags to the following notes to create single eighth notes. Flags always go to the right.

9. Add beams to the following notes to create two eighth notes beamed together.

10. Add a dot behind each of the following half notes to create dotted half notes.

WRITING NOTES on the STAFF

1. Write the number of beats each note receives.

1   1½   4   2   1   3   ½   4   1   2   1   3

♫ **Note:** Always follow the **Stem Rules**.

2. Write the following line notes in the Treble Clef. Use half notes.

Middle C   G   B   E   D   F   Middle C

3. Write the following line notes in the Bass Clef. Use quarter notes.

Middle C   A   G   B   F   D   Middle C

4. Write the following space notes in the Treble Clef. Use single eighth notes.

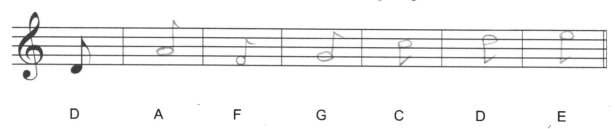

D   A   F   G   C   D   E

5. Write the following space notes in the Bass Clef. Use two eighth notes beamed together.

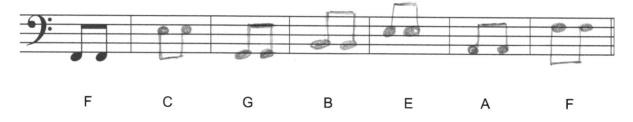

F   C   G   B   E   A   F

REST VALUES

A **REST** symbolizes **SILENCE** in music. Different types of rests indicate the length or duration of silence. A note or rest of the **SAME** name has the **SAME** number of beats.

Each **REST** has a specific time value.

Whole	Half	Quarter	Eighth
Note - Rest	Note - Rest	Note - Rest	Note - Rest
4 beats	2 beats	1 beat	½ beat

♫ **Note:** Rests are written in the **SAME** place in the Treble Clef and in the Bass Clef.

1. Write the number of beats each rest receives.

Beats: _____4_____   _____2_____   _____1_____   ____1/2____

A **whole rest** hangs from line 4. (Walk along line 4, fall in the "hole". ▬)
A whole rest takes up half of space 3.

2. Fill in the whole rest. Draw a whole rest.

A **half rest** sits on line 3. (Half rest looks like a Hat. ▬)
A half rest takes up half of space 3.

3. Fill in the half rest. Draw a half rest.

A **quarter rest** begins in space 4 and ends in space 1.
(Quarter rest looks like a "Z" with a "c" underneath. ⅗)

4. Trace the quarter rest. Draw a quarter rest.

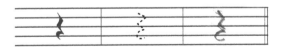

An **eighth rest** begins with a small dot in space 3.
Draw a line up to line 4, then down to space 1.
(Eighth rest looks like the number 7.   )

5. Trace the eighth rest. Draw an eighth rest.

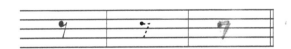

DRAWING RESTS

1. a) A whole rest hangs from line __4__ and falls down into space __3__.
   A whole rest receives __4__ beats.
   b) Draw a whole rest in each measure.

2. a) A half rest sits on line __3__ and goes into space __3__.
   A half rest receives __2__ beats.
   b) Draw a half rest in each measure.

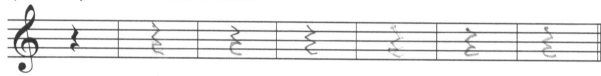

3. a) A quarter rest begins in space __4__. A quarter rest receives __1__ beat.
   b) Draw a quarter rest in each measure.

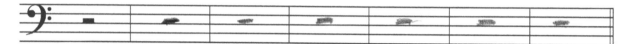

4. a) An eighth rest begins in space __3__. An eighth rest receives __½__ beat.
   b) Draw an eighth rest in each measure.

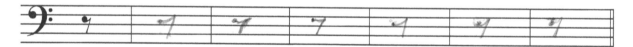

5. Draw a rest that has the same value as each note. Name the rest.

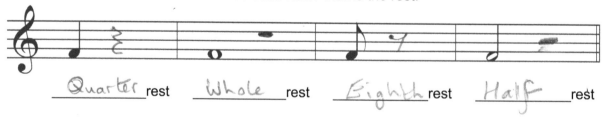

__Quarter__ rest   __Whole__ rest   __Eighth__ rest   __Half__ rest

6. Write the number of beats each note and each rest receives.

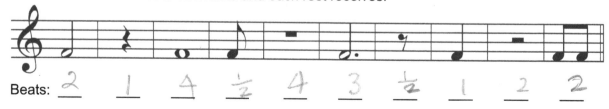

Beats: __2__ __1__ __4__ __½__ __4__ __3__ __½__ __1__ __2__ __2__

Lesson 4   Review Test

1. Draw a **Treble Clef** at the beginning of the staff. Name the notes.

10

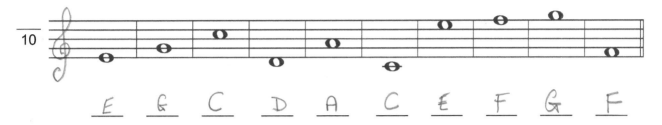

E   G   C   D   A   C   E   F   G   F

2. Draw a **Bass Clef** at the beginning of the staff. Name the notes.

10

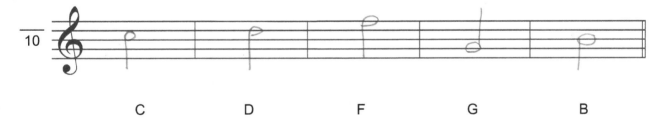

C   F   G   A   B   B   E   C   A   D

3. Write the following notes in the **Treble Clef**. Use **HALF** notes.

10

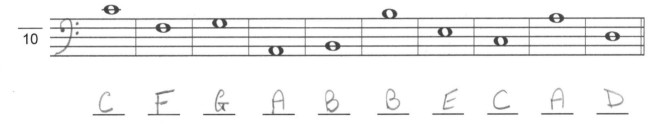

C   D   F   G   B

4. Write the following notes in the **Bass Clef**. Use **DOTTED HALF** notes.

10

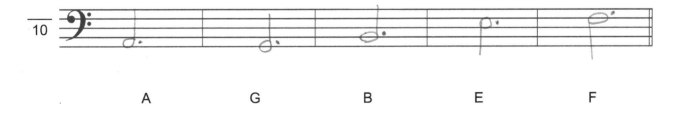

A   G   B   E   F

5. a) Complete the **KEYBOARD** with groups of **TWO** and **THREE black keys**.
b) Write the name of each **WHITE** key directly on the keyboard below.

10

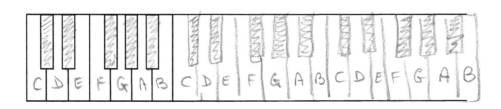

6. Name the following notes in the **BASS Clef**. Circle the **correct pattern** below.

10

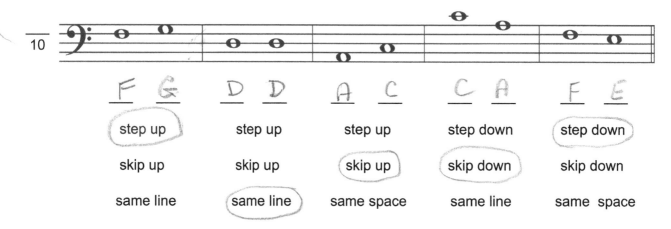

F G	D D	A C	C A	F E
step up	step up	step up	step down	step down
skip up	skip up	skip up	skip down	skip down
same line	same line	same space	same line	same space

7. a) Name the type of **REST**.
b) Write the number of **beats** each rest receives.

10

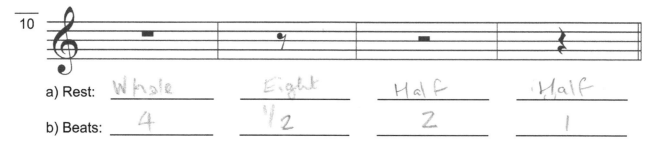

a) Rest: _Whole_   _Eight_   _Half_   _Half_

b) Beats: _4_   _½_   _2_   _1_

8. Add **stems** AND **flags** to the following noteheads to create **EIGHTH** notes. Name the notes.

10

G   C   D   B   D

9. a) Draw a **REST** that has the **SAME** value as each note.
b) Write the number of beats each note and each rest receives.

Beats: ___½___ ___½___ ___4___ ___4___ ___1___ ___1___ ___2___ ___2___

10. Match each musical term with the English definition. (Not all definitions will be used.)

Term		Definition
half rest and whole rest sit in	__j__ ✓	a) receives 1 beat
flag on an eighth note	__c__	b) up on the right or down on the left
half note or half rest	__a__ ✗	c) always goes to the right of the stem
notes on line 3, stems go	__b__ ✓	d) stems go up on the right
whole note or whole rest	__g__ ✓	e) receives 2 beats
quarter note or quarter rest	__e__ ✗	f) stems go down on the left
dotted half note, the dot goes	__i__	g) receives 4 beats
notes below the middle line	__f__ ✓	h) beats
notes above the middle line	__d__ ✗	i) to the right of the note, in the same space for a space note and in the space above for a line note
eighth note or eighth rest	__k__ ✓	j) space 3
		k) receives ½ beat

Lesson 5   Time Signature - Simple Time

A **TIME SIGNATURE** is written on the staff after the clef.

The Staff is divided into **measures** by a **bar line**. Each measure contains an equal number of beats.
A **double bar line** (also called a final bar line) indicates the end of the music.

TWO numbers are used for a **Time Signature**, one above the other.

A Time Signature uses
two spaces for each number.

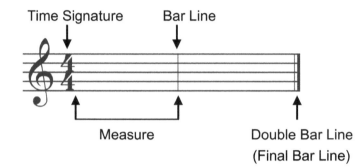

Time Signature   Bar Line

Measure   Double Bar Line
(Final Bar Line)

4   The **TOP NUMBER** indicates how many beats in a measure.
     4 means **FOUR BEATS** per measure.

4   The **BOTTOM NUMBER** indicates what kind of note equals one beat.
     4 means a **QUARTER** note equals **ONE BEAT**.

In $\frac{4}{4}$ time each measure contains 4 beats. A quarter note equals one beat.

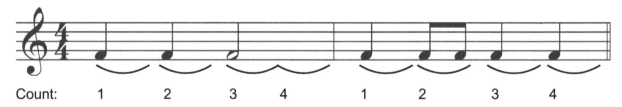

Count: 1   2   3   4   1   2   3   4

1. Add the $\frac{4}{4}$ Time Signature under the bracket. Write the counts below the notes.

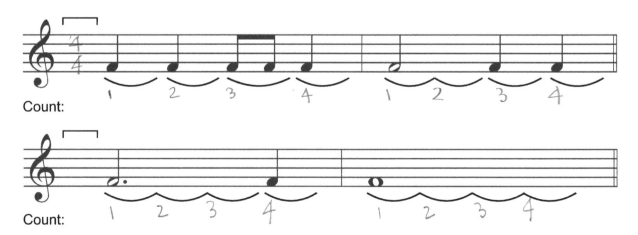

SIMPLE TIME and SCOOPS

In **SIMPLE TIME** the **TOP NUMBER** is: **2**, **3** or **4**.

2 "DUPLE"	**TWO** beats per measure	
3 "TRIPLE"	**THREE** beats per measure	
4 "QUADRUPLE"	**FOUR** beats per measure	

The **BOTTOM NUMBER** is the Basic Beat.

The bottom number **4** indicates that **one quarter note** (♩) is equal to **ONE** Basic Beat.

One **SCOOP** is equal to one Basic Beat (♩). Scoops are a visual representation of the sound or rest "space". Scoops are joined together when note or rest values equal more than one beat.

Counts: 1   1   1   1   1 2   1 2 3   1 2 3 4

1. Following the examples:
   a) Scoop each Basic Beat in each measure.
   b) Write the Basic Beats and the counts below each scoop.
   c) Add the correct Time Signature below the bracket.

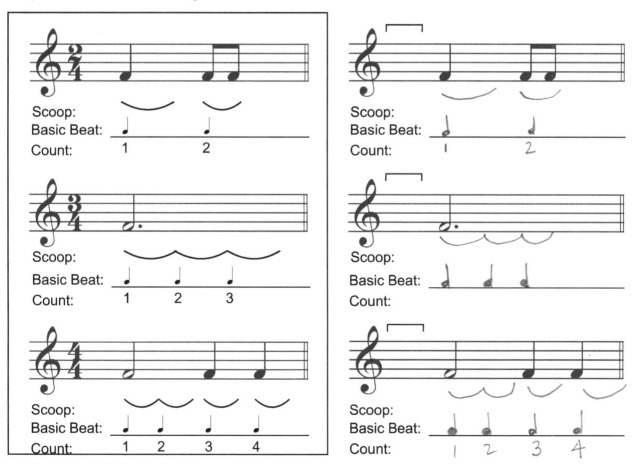

ADDING SIMPLE TIME SIGNATURES

When **ADDING TIME SIGNATURES**, scoop each Basic Beat to determine the number of beats in a measure. Join the scoops together when note or rest values equal more than one beat.

1. For each of the following:
   a) Scoop each Basic Beat in each measure.
   b) Write the Basic Beats and the counts below each scoop.
   c) Add the correct Time Signature below the bracket.

ADDING BAR LINES

When **ADDING BAR LINES**, check the Time Signature to determine how many beats per measure. The bottom number **4** of the Time Signature indicates that a quarter note equals one Basic Beat.

1. For each of the following:
   a) Scoop each Basic Beat in each measure.
   b) Write the Basic Beats and the counts below each scoop.
   c) Add bar lines.

NOTE and REST VALUE REVIEW

1. Write the number of beats each note and each rest receives.

1	1	2	2	4	4	½	½	1	3

2. Add ONE REST below each bracket to complete the following measures with FOUR beats in each measure. Cross off the Basic Beat as each beat is completed.

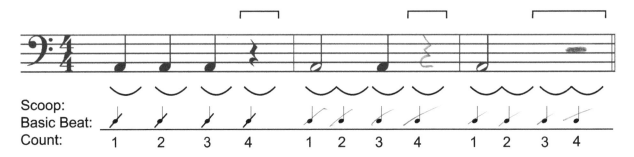

Scoop:
Basic Beat:
Count: 1   2   3   4   1   2   3   4   1   2   3   4

3. Add ONE REST below each bracket to complete the following measures with THREE beats in each measure. Cross off the Basic Beat as each beat is completed.

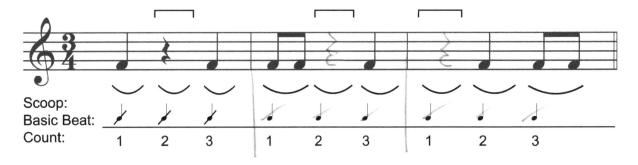

Scoop:
Basic Beat:
Count: 1   2   3   1   2   3   1   2   3

4. Add ONE REST below each bracket to complete the following measures with TWO beats in each measure. Cross off the Basic Beat as each beat is completed.

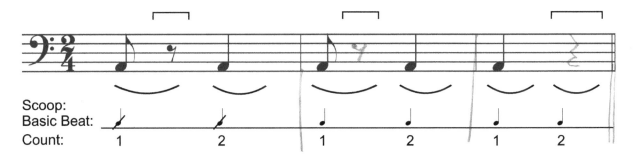

Scoop:
Basic Beat:
Count: 1   2   1   2   1   2

COMPLETING MEASURES with RESTS

The **TOP** number of the **Time Signature** indicates the number of beats in each measure.

1. For each of the following:
   a) Write the number of counts under the Basic Beat for each measure.
   b) Add ONE REST below each bracket to complete the following measures.
   c) Cross off the Basic Beat as each beat is completed.

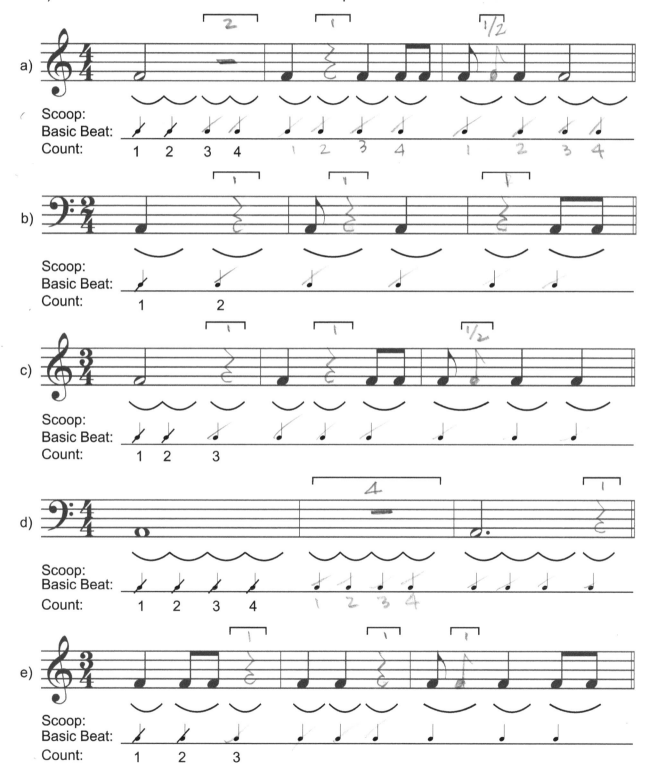

Lesson 5   Review Test

Total Score: ____

/100

1. Name the notes in the **Treble Clef**.

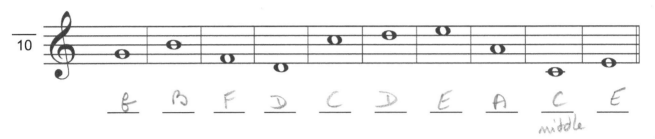

      E   B   F   D   C   D   E   A   C   E

                                                                  middle

2. Write the following notes in the **Bass Clef**. Use **HALF** notes.

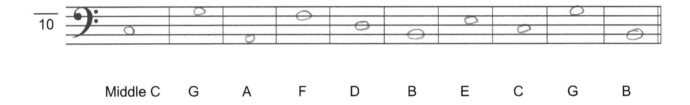

Middle C   G   A   F   D   B   E   C   G   B

3. Write the scoops, Basic Beat and counts below each measure. Add **ONE** rest below each bracket to complete the measure. Cross off the Basic Beat as each beat is completed.

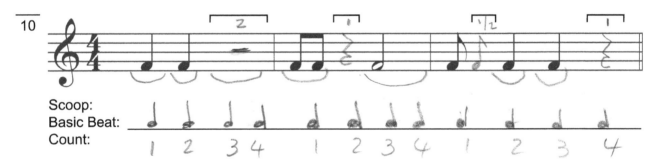

4. Write the scoops, Basic Beat and counts below each measure. Add **bar lines**.

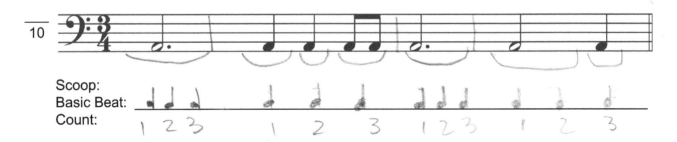

5. Write the scoops, Basic Beat and counts below each measure. Add the correct **Time Signature** below each bracket.

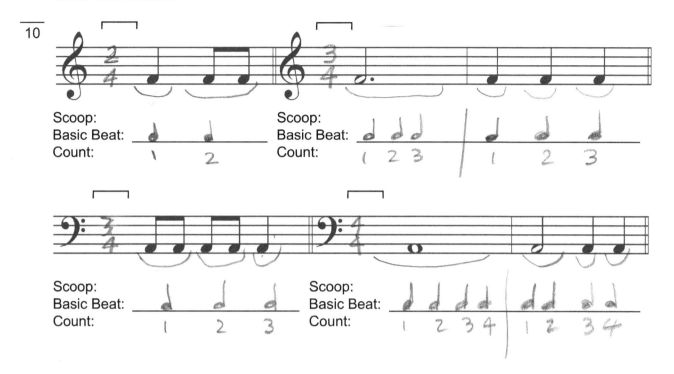

Scoop:
Basic Beat: _____
Count: 1 2

Scoop:
Basic Beat: _____
Count: 1 2 3 | 1 2 3

Scoop:
Basic Beat: _____
Count: 1 2 3

Scoop:
Basic Beat: _____
Count: 1 2 3 4 | 1 2 3 4

6. Name the following notes in the **Treble Clef**. Circle the **correct pattern** below.

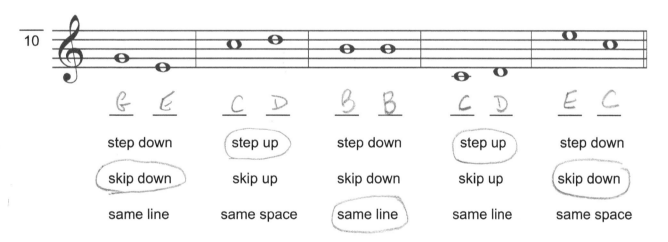

G E   C D   B B   C D   E C

step down   (step up)   step down   (step up)   step down

(skip down)   skip up   skip down   skip up   (skip down)

same line   same space   (same line)   same line   same space

7. Draw a **REST** that has the **SAME** value as each note. Write the number of beats each note and each rest receives.

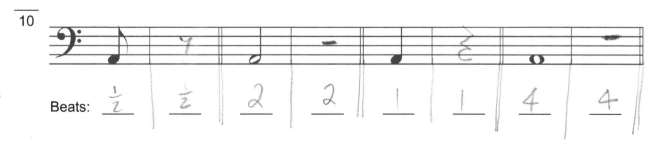

Beats: $\frac{1}{2}$ $\frac{1}{2}$ 2   2   1   1   4   4

8. Add **stems** to the following notes to create **HALF** notes. Name the notes.

10

G   C   D   B   E

9. Fill in the blanks for the **TIME SIGNATURES** below.

10

The TOP number in $\frac{4}{4}$ time indicates __4__ beats in a measure.

The TOP number in $\frac{3}{4}$ time indicates __3__ beats in a measure.

The TOP number in $\frac{2}{4}$ time indicates __2__ beats in a measure.

The BOTTOM number **4** indicates a __crotchet__ note equals __1__ beat.

10. Match each musical term with the English definition. (Not all definitions will be used.)

10

Term		Definition
bottom number **4** of the Time Signature	b	✓a) indicates the end of the music
		b) indicates a quarter note equals one beat
bar line	e	✓c) 3 beats per measure
measure	g	✓d) a unit of musical time in between 2 bar lines
top number of the Time Signature	d	✓e) a vertical line separating music into measures
quarter rest	h	✓f) 2 beats per measure
double bar line	a	✓g) four beats of silence
half rest	k	✓h) one beat of silence
$\frac{2}{4}$ - top number means	f	i) indicates how many beats in a measure
$\frac{3}{4}$ - top number means	c	✓j) 4 beats per measure
$\frac{4}{4}$ - top number means	j	✓k) two beats of silence

Lesson 6   Simple Time - Pulse and Whole Rest

SIMPLE TIME - TOP Number is **2**, **3** or **4**. The top number indicates the number of beats per measure. Each beat has a **PULSE**: **S = Strong   w = weak   M = Medium**

The **PULSE** is where the rhythmic emphasis falls in a measure. Each Basic Beat has a pulse.

Use an **UPPER CASE** letter for **S** (Strong) and **M** (Medium), and use a **lower case** letter for **w** (weak).

Pulse:	**2**	Strong weak	S w
Pulse:	**3**	Strong weak weak	S w w
Pulse:	**4**	Strong weak Medium weak	S w M w

1. Write the pulse below each Basic Beat.

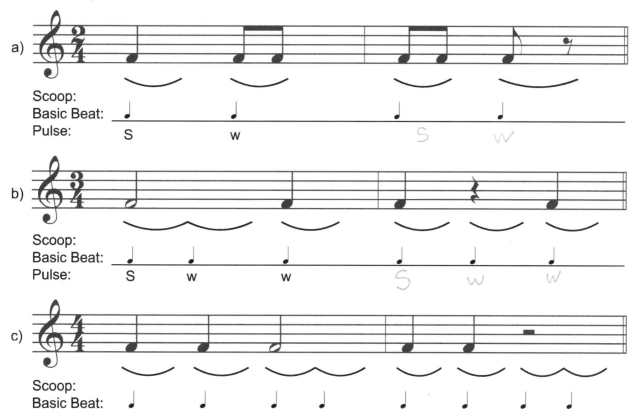

2. Write the pulse for the TOP number of the following Time Signatures:

Pulse:	$\frac{2}{4}$	S	w		
Pulse:	$\frac{3}{4}$	S	w	w	
Pulse:	$\frac{4}{4}$	S	w	M	w

PULSES and WHOLE RESTS in SIMPLE TIME

1. a) Write the pulse below each Basic Beat.
   b) Add ONE REST below each bracket.
   c) Cross off the Basic Beat as each beat is completed.

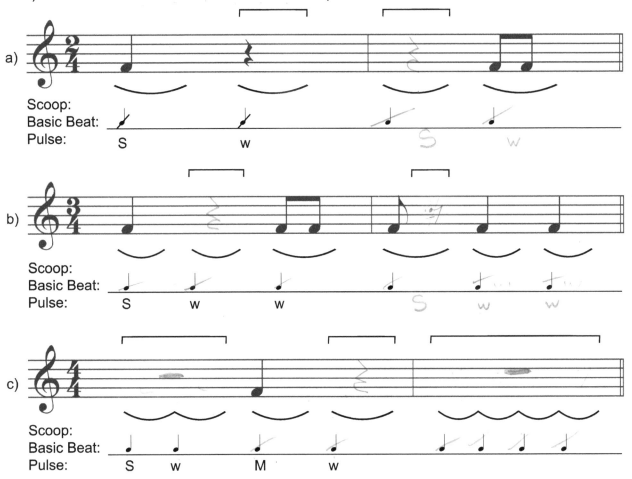

A **WHOLE REST** fills an entire measure of silence in **ANY** Time Signature. The top number of the Time Signature indicates the number of beats given to the whole rest.

♫ **Note:** A whole rest always hangs from line four and falls into space three.

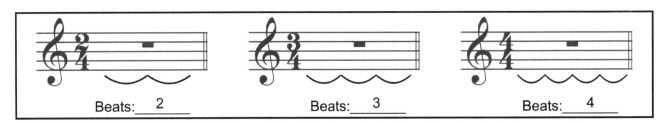

Beats: 2   Beats: 3   Beats: 4

2. Draw a whole rest in each measure. Write the number of beats given to each whole rest.

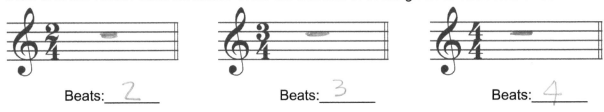

Beats: 2   Beats: 3   Beats: 4

ADDING the PULSE

1. Write the pulse below each Basic Beat. Add bar lines to complete the measures.

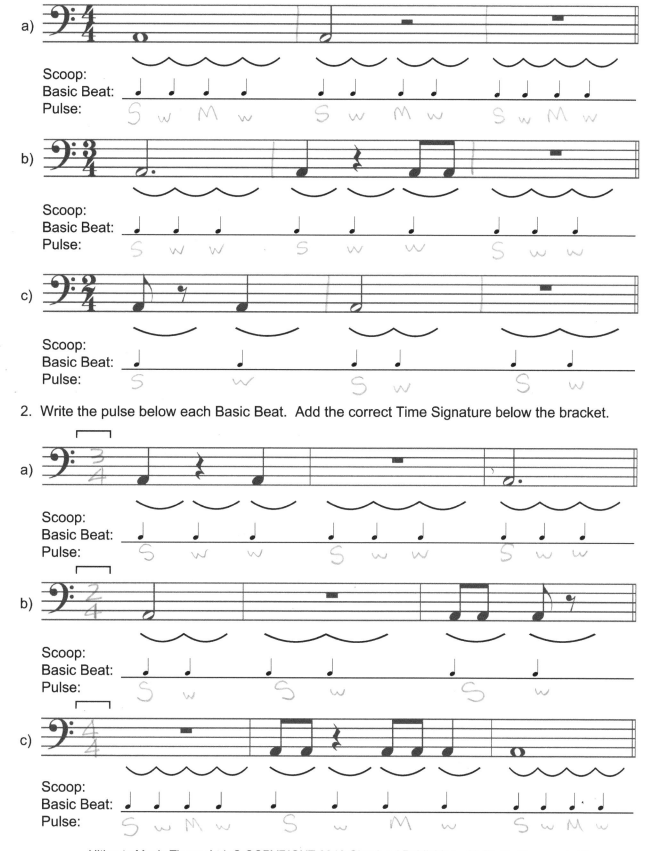

2. Write the pulse below each Basic Beat. Add the correct Time Signature below the bracket.

PULSE: STRONG + weak and MEDIUM + weak

The **plus (+)** sign indicates to **join** the Strong + weak (**S + w**) and the Medium + weak (**M + w**) pulses.

♫ **Note:** A **Strong** beat (pulse) can be combined with a **weak** beat (pulse) into one rest. **S + w**

1. a) Join the **Strong + weak** pulses. Write the scoops below each measure.
   b) Add ONE REST below the bracket to complete each measure.
   c) Cross off the Basic Beat as each beat is completed.

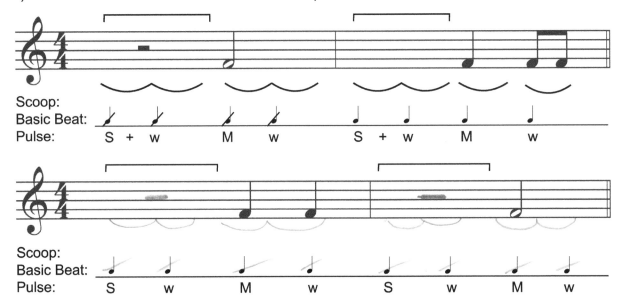

♫ **Note:** A **Medium** beat (pulse) can be combined with a **weak** beat (pulse) into one rest. **M + w**

2. a) Join the **Medium + weak** pulses. Write the scoops below each measure.
   b) Add ONE REST below the bracket to complete each measure.
   c) Cross off the Basic Beat as each beat is completed.

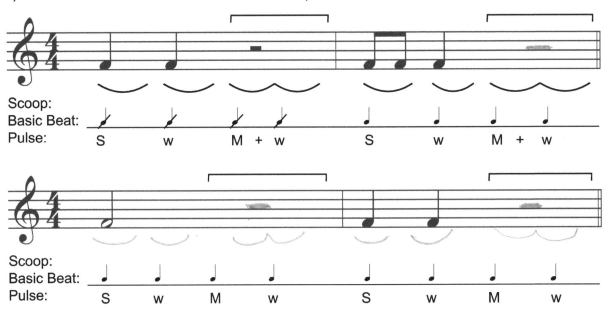

PULSE: weak ~ MEDIUM and weak~ weak

The **tilde** (~) sign (pronounced TILL-day) indicates to **NOT** join the weak ~ Medium (**w ~ M**) pulses or the weak ~ weak (**w ~ w**) pulses.

♫ **Note:** A weak beat (pulse) can NOT be combined with a Medium beat or weak beat.
A weak beat (pulse) always stands alone. **w ~ M or w ~ w**

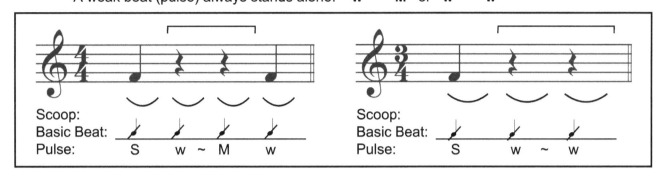

1. Write the correct sign (plus **+** sign or tilde **~** sign) between each of the following pulses.

   a) Strong _____ weak   b) weak _____ weak   c) Medium _____ weak   d) weak _____ Medium

---

REST RULES:
A Strong joins a weak into one rest (**S + w**). A Medium joins a weak into one rest (**M + w**).
A weak can not be joined to a Medium or a weak. It must use 2 separate rests (**w ~ M** and **w ~ w**).

---

2. a) Write the scoops below each measure. Use the "**+**" to join **S + w** and **M + w**, and use ONE rest.
   Use the "**~**" to NOT join **w ~ M** and **w ~ w**, and use TWO separate rests.
   b) Add a rest or rests below the bracket to complete each measure.
   c) Cross off the Basic Beat as each beat is completed.

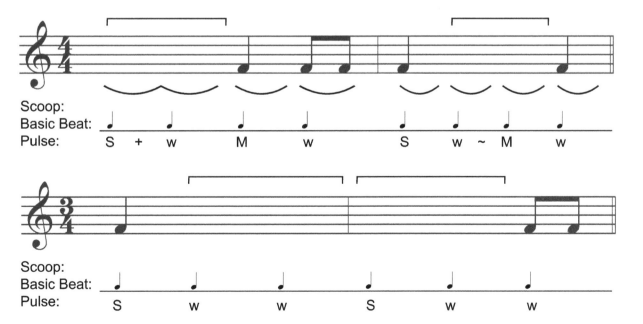

DYNAMICS

DYNAMICS (loud or soft sounds) will vary depending upon the dynamic markings in the music.

Dynamic markings are symbols or signs written in music to indicate different volumes of sound.

Term	Symbol or Sign	Definition
crescendo	*cresc.* or ⟨	becoming louder
diminuendo	*dim.* or	becoming softer
decrescendo	*decresc.* or ⟩	becoming softer
fortissimo	*ff*	very loud
forte	*f*	loud
mezzo forte	*mf*	medium loud (moderately loud)
mezzo piano	*mp*	medium soft (moderately soft)
piano	*p*	soft
pianissimo	*pp*	very soft

1. Write the symbol or sign for each definition (use each symbol or sign only once).

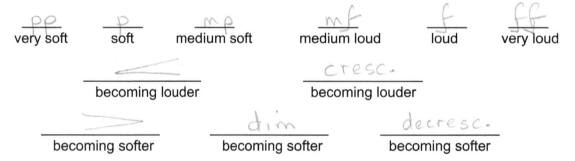

pp	*p*	*mp*	*mf*	*f*	*ff*
very soft	soft	medium soft	medium loud	loud	very loud

⟨	cresc.
becoming louder	becoming louder

⟩	dim	decresc.
becoming softer	becoming softer	becoming softer

Dynamics are written **BELOW** the Treble Clef and **ABOVE** the Bass Clef.

2. Copy the music below, adding the dynamic markings.

Lesson 6   Review Test

Total Score: ____
100

1. Name the notes in the **Bass Clef**.

A   F   G   E   G   D   B   B   A   C

2. Write the following notes in the **Treble Clef**. Use **HALF** notes.

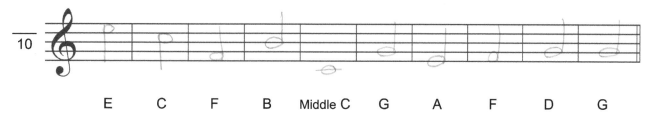

E   C   F   B   Middle C   G   A   F   D   G

3. Scoop each beat. Write the pulse below each Basic Beat. Add **RESTS** below each bracket to complete the measure. Cross off the Basic Beat as each beat is completed.

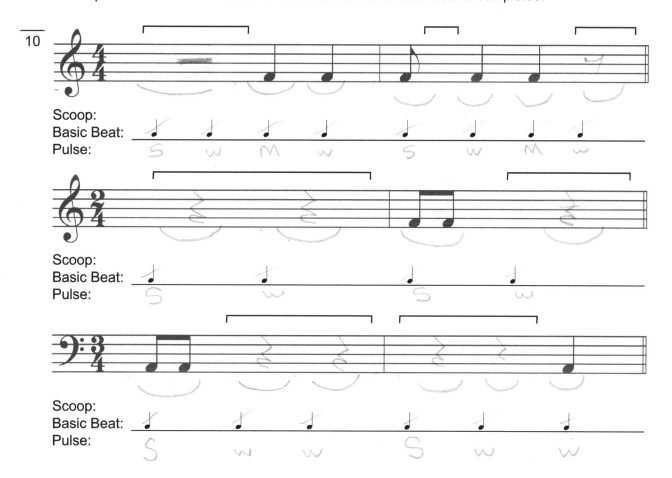

4. Write the scoops, Basic Beats and pulse below each measure. Add **bar lines**.

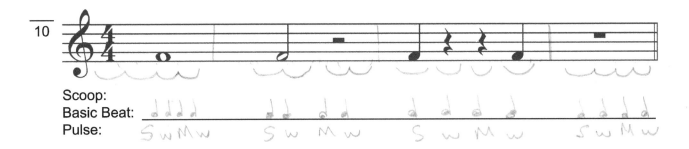

Scoop:
Basic Beat:
Pulse:

5. Write the scoops, Basic Beats and pulse below each measure. Add the correct **Time Signature** below each bracket.

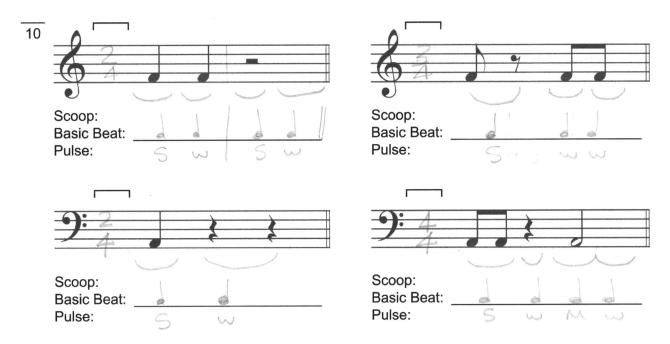

Scoop:
Basic Beat:
Pulse:

Scoop:
Basic Beat:
Pulse:

Scoop:
Basic Beat:
Pulse:

Scoop:
Basic Beat:
Pulse:

6. Name the following notes in the **Bass Clef**. Circle the **correct pattern** below.

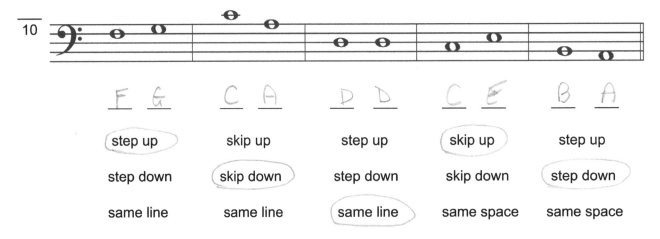

F G   C A   D D   C E   B A

step up	skip up	step up	skip up	step up
step down	skip down	step down	skip down	step down
same line	same line	same line	same space	same space

7. Draw a **REST** that has the **SAME** value as each note. Write the number of beats each note and each rest receives.

Beats: _1_ _1_ _4_ _4_ _½_ _½_ _2_ _2_

8. Add a **DOT** to each of the following notes to create **DOTTED HALF** notes. Name the notes.

_G_ _C_ _A_ _F_ _B_

9. Circle **Correct** if the **+** and **scoops** show the correct grouping when joining two Basic Beats into one rest. Circle **Incorrect** if it does not.

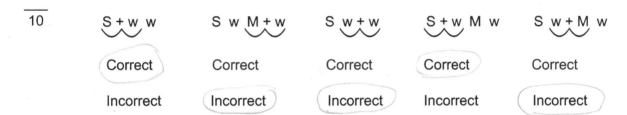

S + w w   S w M + w   S w + w   S + w M w   S w + M w

(Correct)   Correct   Correct   (Correct)   Correct

Incorrect   (Incorrect)   (Incorrect)   Incorrect   (Incorrect)

10. Match each musical term or sign with the English definition. (Not all definitions will be used.)

Term		Definition
piano, *p*	_d_ ✓	a) becoming louder
forte, *f*	_f_ ✓	b) moderately soft
crescendo, cresc.	_a_ ✓	c) very loud
dynamics	_i_ ✓	d) soft
diminuendo, dim.	_h_ ✓	e) very soft
decrescendo, decresc.	_k_ ✓	f) loud
fortissimo, *ff*	_c_ ✓	g) moderately loud
pianissimo, *pp*	_e_ ✓	h) becoming softer
mezzo forte, *mf*	_g_ ✓	i) indicates volume of sound (loud or soft)
mezzo piano, *mp*	_b_ ✓	j) slowly
		k) becoming softer

Lesson 7   Semitones or Half Steps and Accidentals

A **SEMITONE or HALF STEP** is the shortest distance between two neighbouring (next door) keys on the keyboard, black or white, no key in between. A semitone (half step) is indicated by an **ST**.

♫ **Note:** A semitone can go from a white key to a black key, from a black key to a white key, or from a white key to a white key. A semitone can never go from a black key to a black key.

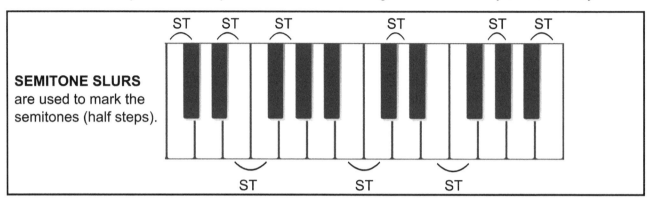

An **ACCIDENTAL** is a sign that raises or lowers the pitch one semitone (half step).

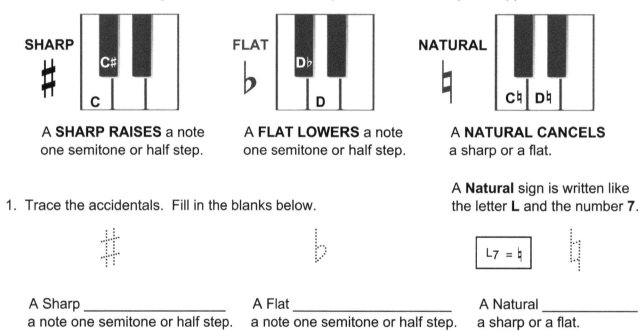

A **SHARP RAISES** a note one semitone or half step.

A **FLAT LOWERS** a note one semitone or half step.

A **NATURAL CANCELS** a sharp or a flat.

A **Natural** sign is written like the letter **L** and the number **7**.

1. Trace the accidentals. Fill in the blanks below.

L7 = ♮

A Sharp _____ a note one semitone or half step.

A Flat _____ a note one semitone or half step.

A Natural _____ a sharp or a flat.

2. A _____ or _____ is the shortest distance between two neighbouring keys on the keyboard, black or white, no key in between.

3. Label the following accidental signs as sharp, flat or natural.

_____   _____   _____   _____   _____   _____

ACCIDENTALS

An **ACCIDENTAL** only applies to the notes on the line or in the space where it is written. It does NOT apply to notes that have the same letter name but appear on a higher or lower position on the staff. An accidental is cancelled by either another accidental or a bar line.

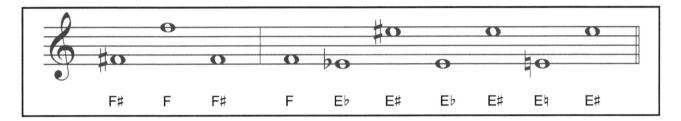

♫ **Note:** An accidental is written **IN FRONT** of a note to raise or lower the pitch.
An accidental is written **AFTER** the letter name.

1. Name the following notes.

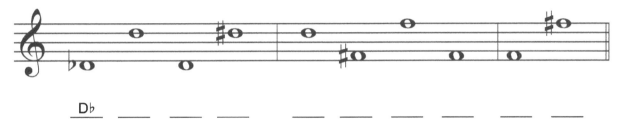

D♭ ___ ___ ___ ___ ___ ___ ___

♫ **Note:** When a **NATURAL** sign is written in front of the note, a natural sign must appear after the letter name. Once the note has been made a natural, the natural sign is NOT needed for any note repeated on the same line or in the same space within that measure.

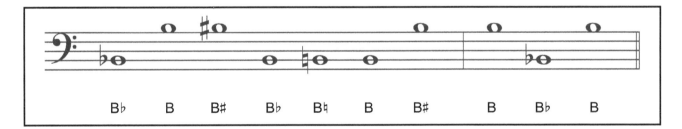

B♭ B B♯ B♭ B♮ B B♯ B B♭ B

♫ **Note:** A bar line **CANCELS** an accidental.

2. Name the following notes.

F♯ ___ ___ ___ ___ ___ ___ ___

SHARP ♯

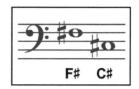

F♯ C♯

A **SHARP RAISES** a note one semitone (half step),
using the **SAME** letter name.

The sharp sign is written **IN FRONT** of the note and **AFTER** the letter name.
A sharp can be a black or white key.

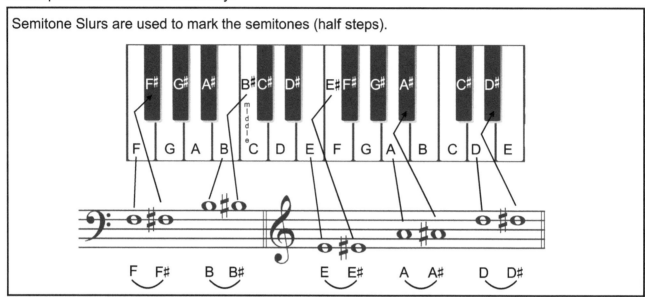

Semitone Slurs are used to mark the semitones (half steps).

A **SHARP** sign is written **IN FRONT** of the note. The **middle** of the sharp must be in the **same space** for a space note, or on the **same line** for a line note.

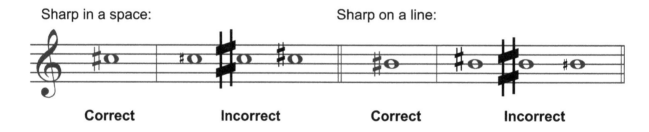

Sharp in a space: Sharp on a line:

Correct   **Incorrect**   **Correct**   **Incorrect**

1. Write a SHARP in front of the following SPACE notes. Name the notes.

F♯   _____   _____   _____   _____   _____

2. Write a SHARP in front of the following LINE notes. Name the notes.

F♯   _____   _____   _____   _____   _____

3. Draw a line from each note on the staff to the corresponding key on the keyboard (at the correct pitch). Name the notes.

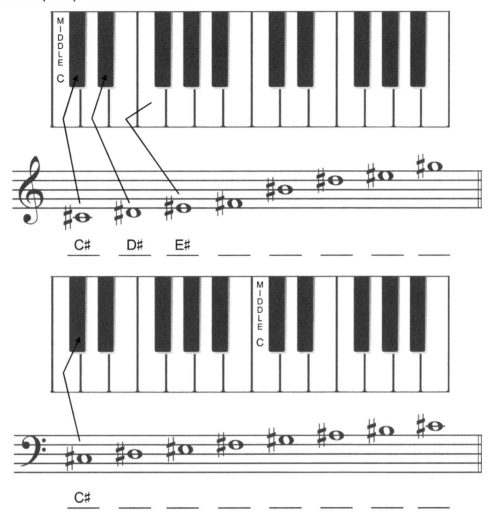

C#   D#   E#   ___   ___   ___   ___   ___

C#   ___   ___   ___   ___   ___   ___   ___

4. a) Write the following SHARP notes in the Treble Clef for each key marked with a ☺.
   b) Draw a line from each note on the staff to the corresponding key on the keyboard (at the correct pitch).
   c) Name the notes.

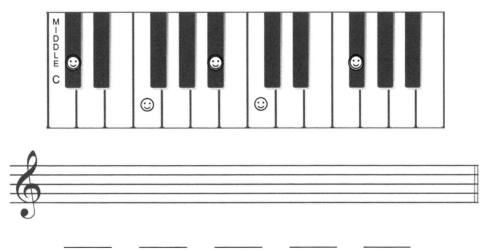

___   ___   ___   ___   ___

FLAT ♭

A **FLAT LOWERS** a note one semitone (half step), using the **SAME** letter name.

The flat sign is written **IN FRONT** of the note and **AFTER** the letter name.
A flat can be a black or white key.

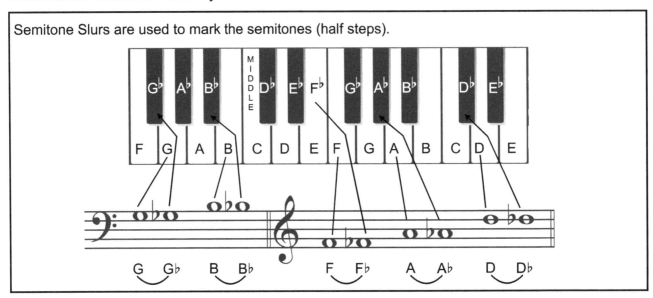

Semitone Slurs are used to mark the semitones (half steps).

A **FLAT** sign is written **IN FRONT** of the note. The **middle** of the flat must be in the **same space** for a space note, or on the **same line** for a line note.

Flat in a space: Flat on a line:

Correct   Incorrect   Correct   Incorrect

1. Write a FLAT in front of the following SPACE notes. Name the notes.

B♭   ___   ___   ___   ___   ___

2. Write a FLAT in front of the following LINE notes. Name the notes.

B♭   ___   ___   ___   ___   ___

3. Draw a line from each note on the staff to the corresponding key on the keyboard (at the correct pitch). Name the notes.

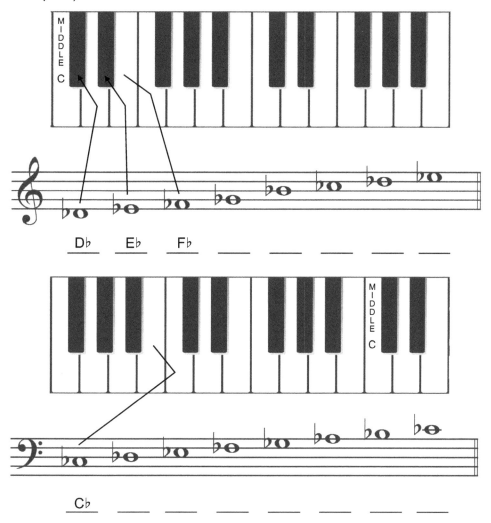

Db   Eb   Fb   ___   ___   ___   ___

Cb   ___   ___   ___   ___   ___   ___

4. a) Write the following FLAT notes in the Treble Clef for each key marked with a ☺.
   b) Draw a line from each note on the staff to the corresponding key on the keyboard (at the correct pitch).
   c) Name the notes.

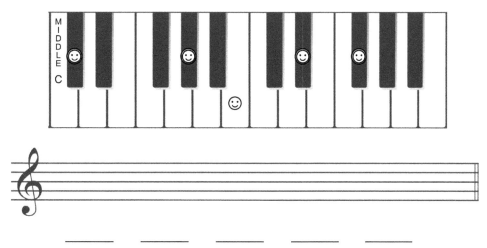

___   ___   ___   ___   ___

NATURAL ♮

A **NATURAL SIGN CANCELS** a sharp or flat.

A natural sign **lowers a sharp** one semitone (half step) or
raises a flat one semitone (half step), using the **SAME** letter name.

The natural sign is written **IN FRONT** of the note and **AFTER** the letter name.
A natural is ALWAYS a white key.

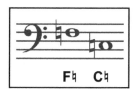

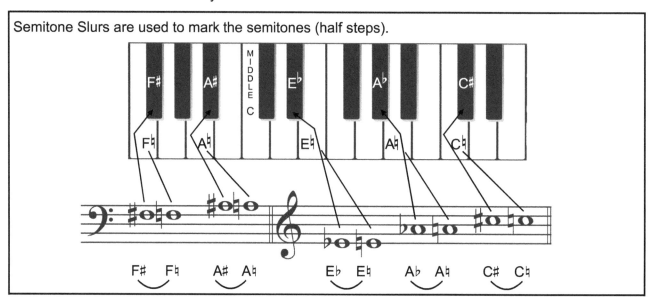

Semitone Slurs are used to mark the semitones (half steps).

A **NATURAL** sign is written **IN FRONT** of the note. The **middle** of the natural sign must be in the **same space** for a space note, or on the **same line** for a line note.

♫ **Note:** The **NATURAL** sign is written like the letter **L** and the number **7**.

L7 = ♮

Natural in a space: Natural on a line:

Correct   **Incorrect**   **Correct**   **Incorrect**

1. Write a NATURAL in front of the following SPACE notes. Name the notes.

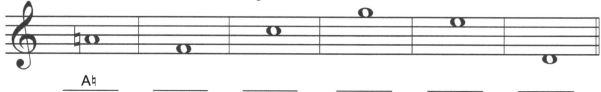

___A♮___   _____   _____   _____   _____

2. Write a NATURAL in front of the following LINE notes. Name the notes.

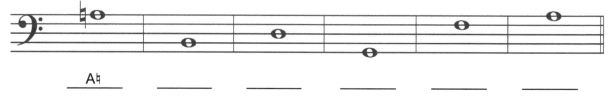

___A♮___   _____   _____   _____   _____

3. Draw a line from each note on the staff to the corresponding key on the keyboard (at the correct pitch). Name the notes.

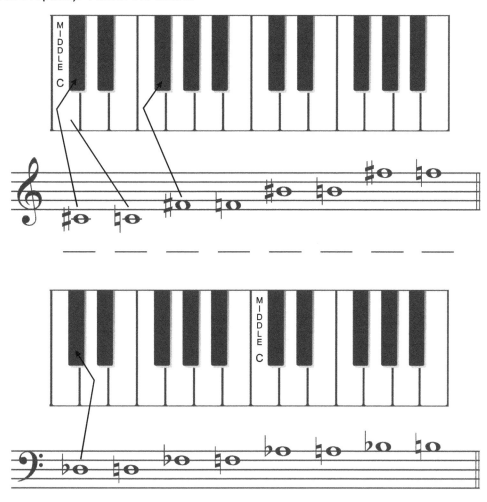

4. a) Write a NATURAL sign in front of the second note in each measure.
   b) Draw a line from each note on the staff to the corresponding key on the keyboard (at the correct pitch).
   c) Name the notes.

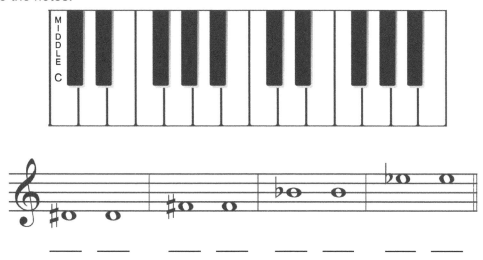

Lesson 7   Review Test

1. Name the notes in the **Treble Clef**. Draw a line from each note on the staff to the corresponding key on the keyboard (at the correct pitch).

10

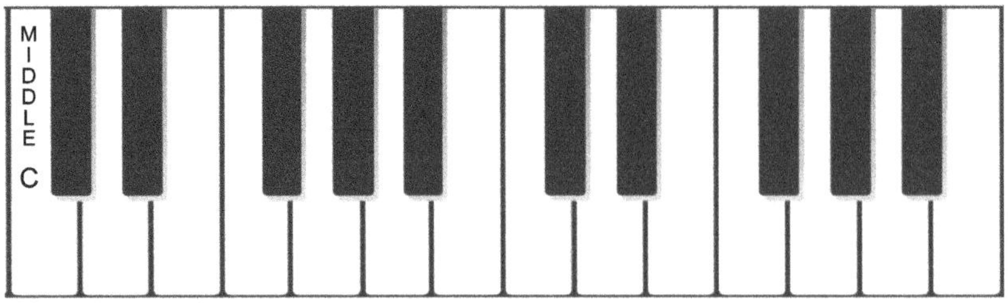

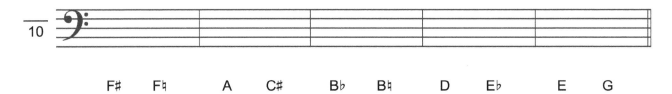

2. Write the following notes in the **Bass Clef**. Use **WHOLE** notes.

10

F♯   F♮   A   C♯   B♭   B♮   D   E♭   E   G

3. Scoop each beat. Write the pulse below each Basic Beat. Add **RESTS** below each bracket to complete the measure. Cross off the Basic Beat as each beat is completed.

10

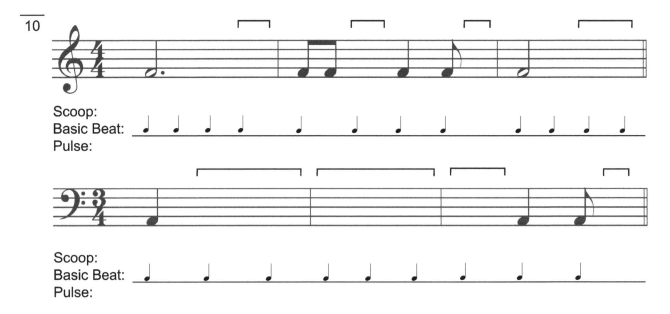

Scoop:
Basic Beat:
Pulse:

Scoop:
Basic Beat:
Pulse:

74

4. Write the scoops, Basic Beat and pulse below each measure. Add **bar lines**.

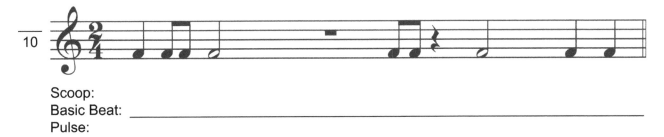

Scoop:
Basic Beat: _____
Pulse:

5. Write the scoops, Basic Beat and pulse below each measure. Add the correct **Time Signature** below each bracket.

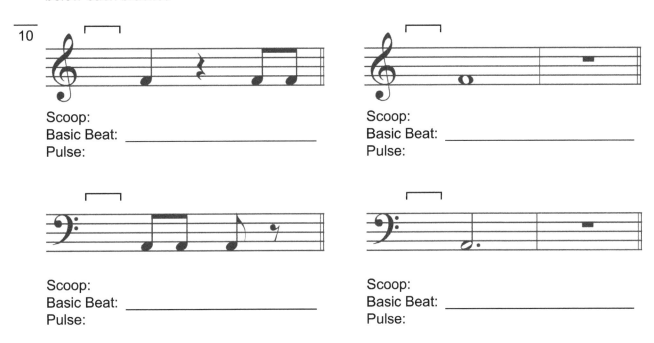

Scoop:
Basic Beat: _____
Pulse:

Scoop:
Basic Beat: _____
Pulse:

Scoop:
Basic Beat: _____
Pulse:

Scoop:
Basic Beat: _____
Pulse:

6. Name the notes in the **Bass Clef**. Circle the **correct pattern** below.

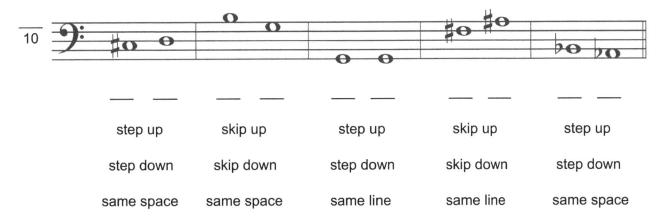

step up	skip up	step up	skip up	step up
step down	skip down	step down	skip down	step down
same space	same space	same line	same line	same space

7. Write a **NATURAL** in front of the **second** note in each measure. Name the notes.

10

—— ——   —— ——   —— ——   —— ——   —— ——

8. **LOWER** each note a semitone (half step) by writing a FLAT in front of each note.
Name the notes.

10

—— ——   —— ——   —— ——   —— ——   —— ——

9. **RAISE** each note a semitone (half step) by writing a SHARP in front of each note.
Name the notes.

10

—— ——   —— ——   —— ——   —— ——   —— ——

10. Match each musical term with the English definition. (Not all definitions will be used.)

10

Term		Definition
semitone (half step)	_____	a) Strong weak Medium weak
pulse in $\frac{4}{4}$ time	_____	b) one quarter note equals one Basic Beat
flat	_____	c) sharp, flat or natural sign placed in front of a note
accidental	_____	d) cancels a sharp or a flat
pulse in $\frac{3}{4}$ time	_____	e) raises a note one semitone (half step)
sharp	_____	f) Strong weak
natural sign	_____	g) fills an entire measure of silence
pulse in $\frac{2}{4}$ time	_____	h) lowers a note one semitone (half step)
whole rest	_____	i) volume (loud or soft) of sound
bottom number of $\frac{2}{4}$, $\frac{3}{4}$ or $\frac{4}{4}$ Time Signature	_____	j) Strong weak weak
		k) shortest distance between two neighbouring keys on the keyboard

Lesson 8   Whole Tones, Major Pentascales and Triads

A **WHOLE TONE** or **WHOLE STEP** (also called a **TONE**) is equal to **TWO** semitones (half steps).
A whole tone is the distance from one key to another (black or white), with one key in between.
A whole tone (whole step) is indicated by a **WT**.

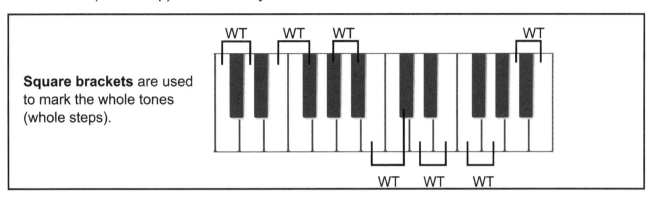

Square brackets are used to mark the whole tones (whole steps).

A **whole tone** (whole step) is written as a step (line note to space note, or space note to line note) and uses neighbouring letter names. Example: C to D, C# to D#, A♭ to B♭, E to F#, E♭ to F.

The distance between the notes in each measure is a whole tone (whole step).

1. Draw a line from each note on the staff to the corresponding key on the keyboard.
   Name the notes.

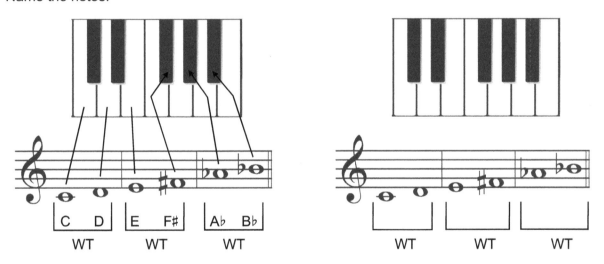

2. Label the distances between the white keys on the keyboard.
   Use a square bracket and the letters **WT** for a **whole tone** (whole step).
   Use a slur and the letters **ST** for a **semitone** (half step).

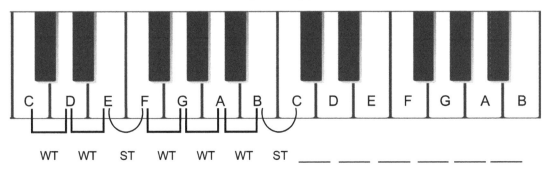

WT   WT   ST   WT   WT   WT   ST   ___ ___ ___ ___ ___ ___

MAJOR PENTASCALE - TONIC

A **MAJOR PENTASCALE** (penta means 5) is a series of 5 notes or degrees in alphabetical order.

A **caret** sign " ^ " (or hat) above a number ($\hat{3}$) indicates the degree number of the scale.

A Major pentascale uses the following pattern:

$\hat{1}$ |whole tone| $\hat{2}$ |whole tone| $\hat{3}$ semitone $\hat{4}$ |whole tone| $\hat{5}$
      WT   WT   ST   WT

♫ **Note:** In the Major pentascale, the semitone (half step) is always between the 3rd and 4th degrees.

The first note ($\hat{1}$) or degree of a pentascale is called the **TONIC**. The Tonic names the pentascale.

1. a) Copy the following Major pentascales. Use whole notes.
   b) Draw a line from each note on the staff to the corresponding key on the keyboard.
   c) Mark the semitone (half step) with a slur. Name the Tonic. Name the Major pentascale.

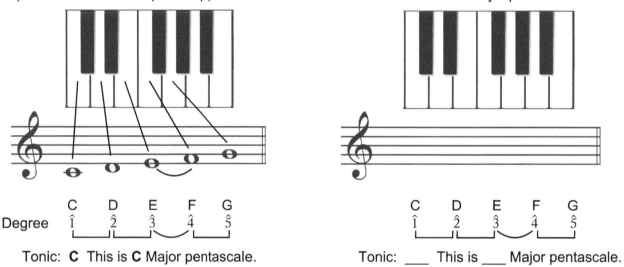

Degree C $\hat{1}$ D $\hat{2}$ E $\hat{3}$ F $\hat{4}$ G $\hat{5}$ C $\hat{1}$ D $\hat{2}$ E $\hat{3}$ F $\hat{4}$ G $\hat{5}$

Tonic: **C** This is **C** Major pentascale.   Tonic: ___ This is ___ Major pentascale.

♫ **Note:** An **accidental** may be needed to complete the Major pentascale pattern.

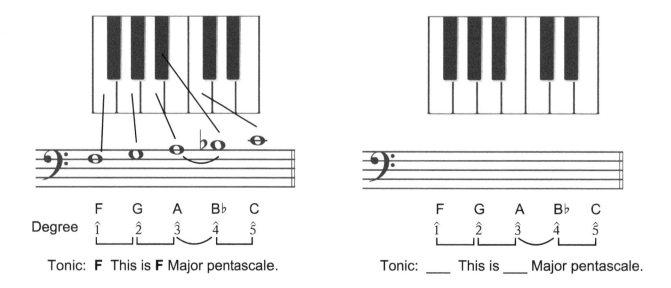

Degree F $\hat{1}$ G $\hat{2}$ A $\hat{3}$ B♭ $\hat{4}$ C $\hat{5}$ F $\hat{1}$ G $\hat{2}$ A $\hat{3}$ B♭ $\hat{4}$ C $\hat{5}$

Tonic: **F** This is **F** Major pentascale.   Tonic: ___ This is ___ Major pentascale.

MAJOR PENTASCALE - TONIC and DOMINANT

In a **MAJOR PENTASCALE**, the **TONIC** is the first ($\hat{1}$) note and the **DOMINANT** is the fifth ($\hat{5}$) note.

1. a) Copy the following Major pentascale. Use whole notes.
   b) Draw a line from each note on the staff to the corresponding key on the keyboard.
   c) Mark the semitone (half step) with a slur. Name the Tonic (first) and Dominant (fifth) notes.

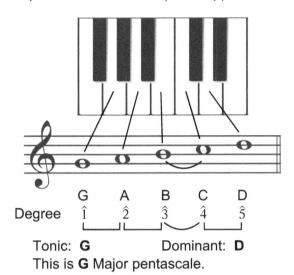

Degree $\hat{1}$ $\hat{2}$ $\hat{3}$ $\hat{4}$ $\hat{5}$

Tonic: **G**   Dominant: **D**
This is **G** Major pentascale.

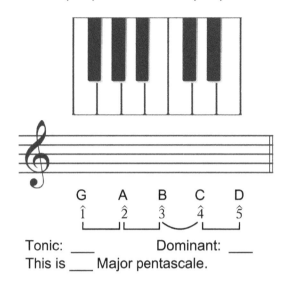

Degree $\hat{1}$ $\hat{2}$ $\hat{3}$ $\hat{4}$ $\hat{5}$

Tonic: ___   Dominant: ___
This is ___ Major pentascale.

♫ **Note:** Roman Numerals are used to identify the Tonic (**I**) and the Dominant (**V**) notes.

2. a) Following the example, name each note of the Major pentascales below.
   b) Use Roman Numerals to label the Tonic (**I**) and the Dominant (**V**) notes.
   c) Name the Major pentascale.

a) G   A   B   C   D

b) I   V   c) This is ___G___ Major pentascale.

a) ___ ___ ___ ___ ___

b) ___   ___   c) This is _____ Major pentascale.

a) ___ ___ ___ ___ ___

b) ___   ___   c) This is _____ Major pentascale.

MAJOR TONIC TRIAD - TONIC, MEDIANT and DOMINANT

A **MAJOR TONIC TRIAD** is a three note chord using the following degrees of the Major pentascale: Tonic (first) $\hat{1}$, Mediant (third) $\hat{3}$, and Dominant (fifth) $\hat{5}$. ALL LINE notes or ALL SPACE notes.

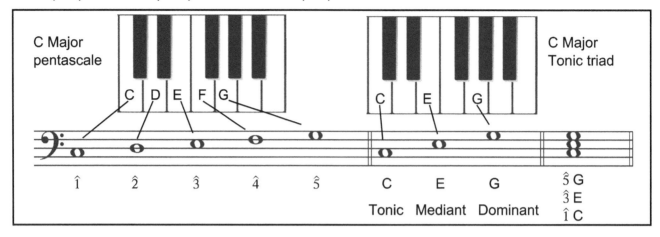

1. Complete the following for G Major and F Major. Use whole notes.
   a) Write the Major pentascale, ascending, in the Bass Clef. Draw a line from each note to the corresponding key on the keyboard. Name the notes directly on the keyboard.
   b) Write the Tonic, Mediant and Dominant notes. Name the notes. Draw a line from each note to the corresponding key on the keyboard. Name the notes directly on the keyboard.
   c) Write the 3 notes of the Major Tonic triad. All line notes or all space notes, one above the other.

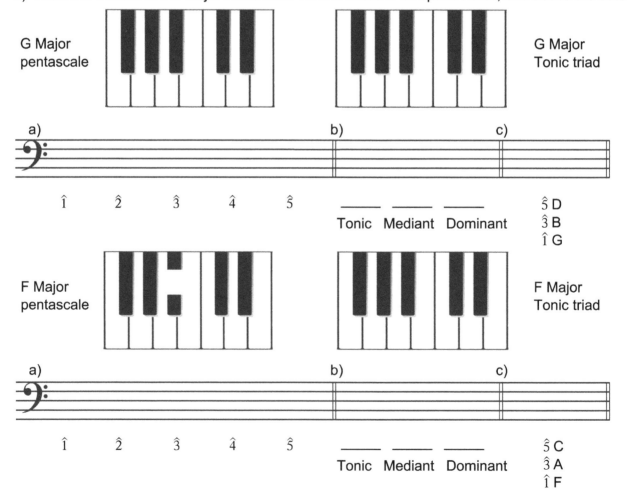

PENTASCALES - ASCENDING and DESCENDING and MAJOR TRIADS

PENTASCALES may be written **ASCENDING** and **DESCENDING**. A center bar line is used after the highest note, the Dominant. Roman Numerals are used to label the Tonic (**I**) and the Dominant (**V**).

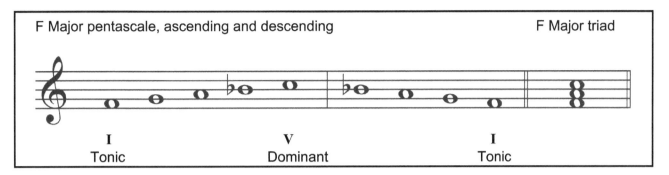

♫ **Note:** If the pentascale contains an accidental, the accidental is repeated after the bar line.

1. a) Write the following Major pentascales, ascending and descending, using accidentals when necessary. Use whole notes.
   b) Use Roman Numerals to label the Tonic (**I**) and the Dominant (**V**) notes.
   c) Write the Major Tonic triad. (All lines or all spaces.) Use whole notes.

a) F Major pentascale

b) _____   _____   _____   c) F Major triad

a) C Major pentascale

b) _____   _____   _____   c) C Major triad

a) G Major pentascale

b) _____   _____   _____   c) G Major triad

SOLID MAJOR TRIADS

The lowest note of a **SOLID MAJOR TRIAD** in root position (all lines or all spaces) is called the root. The root names the triad. In the Tonic triad the lowest note is also called the Tonic (first) note.

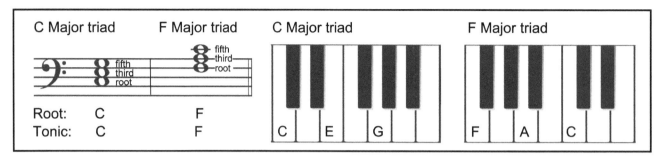

♫ **Note:** A **SOLID** (blocked) triad is written one note **ABOVE** the other.

1. Name the root (lowest note) for each of the following Major triads.

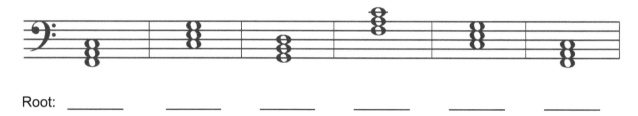

Root: _____   _____   _____   _____   _____   _____

2. Complete the following Major triads by adding the third note and the fifth note above each of the given Tonic notes. Use whole notes. Name the Tonic note.

Tonic: _____   _____   _____   _____   _____   _____

3. Write the note names for each of the following Major triads directly on the keyboard.

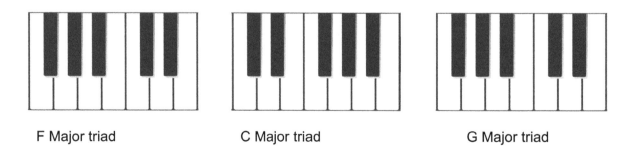

F Major triad   C Major triad   G Major triad

BROKEN MAJOR TRIADS

The lowest note of a **BROKEN MAJOR TRIAD** in root position (all lines or all spaces) is called the root. The root names the triad. In the Tonic triad the lowest note is also called the Tonic (first) note.

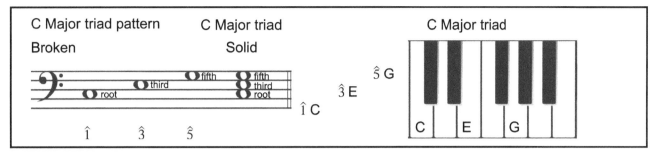

♫ **Note:** A **BROKEN** triad is written one note **BESIDE** the other.

1. a) Name the Tonic note for each of the following Major triads.
   b) Circle Broken or Solid for each of the following Major triads.

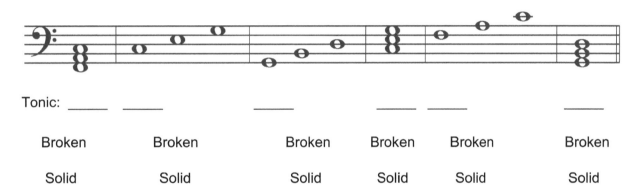

Tonic: _____ _____   _____   _____ _____   _____

| Broken | Broken | Broken | Broken | Broken | Broken |
| Solid | Solid | Solid | Solid | Solid | Solid |

♫ **Note:** When the Tonic note is first, the pattern for the broken root position triad is skipping up.

2. Complete the following broken Major triads by adding the third note and the fifth note beside each of the given Tonic notes. Use whole notes. Name each note.

C Major triad   G Major triad   F Major triad

$\hat{1}$ $\hat{3}$ $\hat{5}$ $\hat{1}$ $\hat{3}$ $\hat{5}$ $\hat{1}$ $\hat{3}$ $\hat{5}$

_____ _____ _____   _____ _____ _____   _____ _____ _____

3. A triad written one note BESIDE the other is called a _____ triad.

4. A triad written one note ABOVE the other is called a _____ triad.

Lesson 8 Review Test

Total Score: ____
100

1. Draw a **Bass Clef** on the staff below. Name the notes.

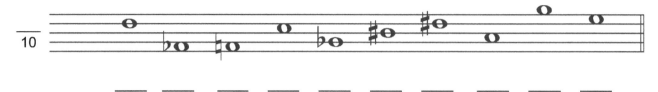

10

_____ _____ _____ _____ _____ _____ _____ _____ _____ _____

2. Draw a **Treble Clef** on the staff below. Write the following notes in the Treble Clef.
Use whole notes.

10

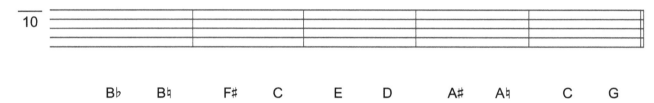

B♭   B♮   F#   C   E   D   A#   A♮   C   G

3. Scoop each beat. Write the pulse below each Basic Beat. Add **RESTS** below each bracket
to complete the measure. Cross off the Basic Beat as each beat is completed.

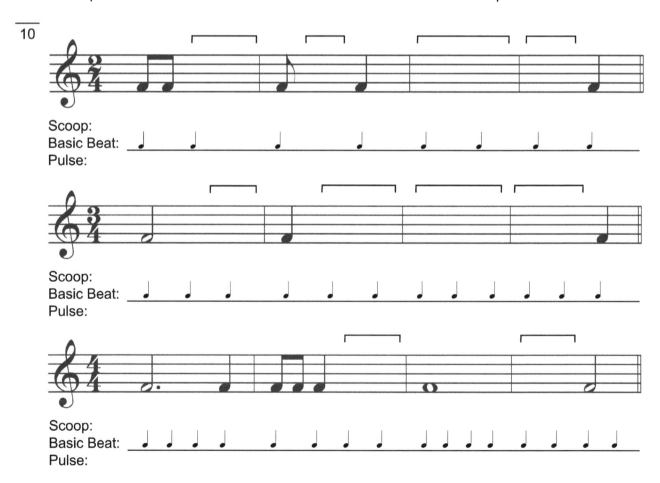

10

Scoop:
Basic Beat:
Pulse:

Scoop:
Basic Beat:
Pulse:

Scoop:
Basic Beat:
Pulse:

4. Write the scoops, Basic Beat and pulse below each measure. Add **bar lines**.

10

Scoop:
Basic Beat: _____
Pulse:

5. a) Write the following Major pentascales, ascending and descending, using accidentals when necessary. Use whole notes.
b) Use Roman Numerals to label the Tonic (**I**) and the Dominant (**V**) notes.

10 c) Write the solid Major Tonic triad. (All lines or all spaces.) Use whole notes. Name the triad.

a) C Major pentascale

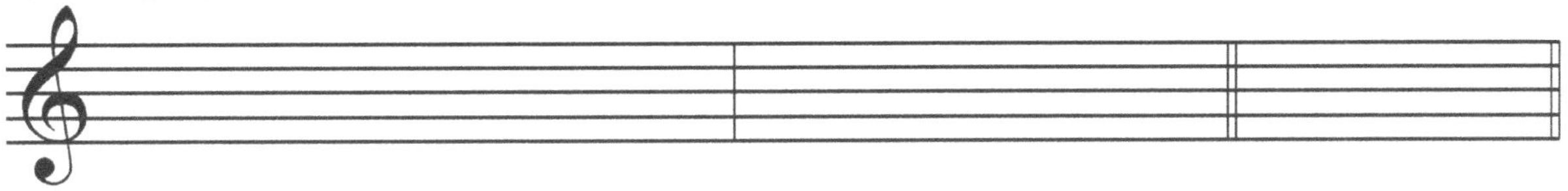

b) _____   _____   _____   c) _____ Major triad

a) G Major pentascale

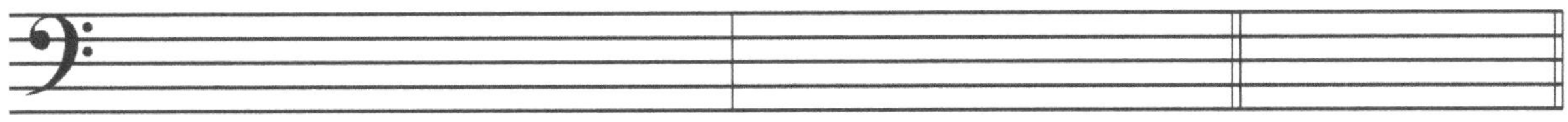

b) _____   _____   _____   c) _____ Major triad

a) F Major pentascale

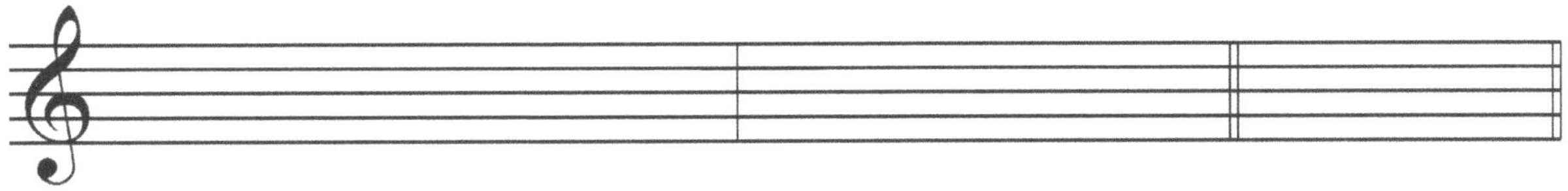

b) _____   _____   _____   c) _____ Major triad

6. Name the notes. Circle whole tone (whole step) or semitone (half step) for each of the following.

10

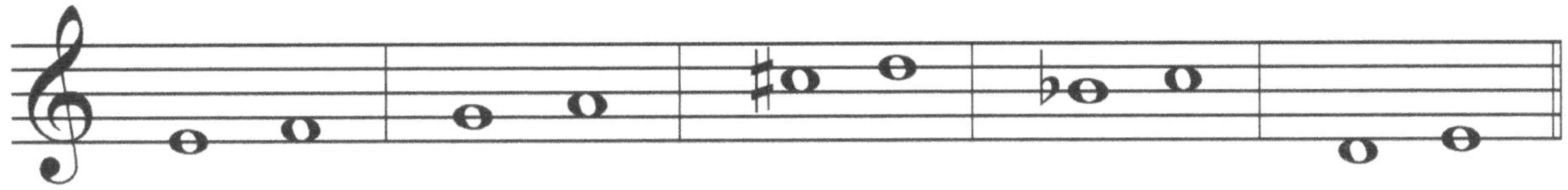

___ ___   ___ ___   ___ ___   ___ ___   ___ ___

whole tone   whole tone   whole tone   whole tone   whole tone

semitone   semitone   semitone   semitone   semitone

7. Using accidentals, **LOWER** the following notes a semitone (half step).
   Use the **SAME** letter name. Use whole notes. Name the notes.

10

___ ___ ___ ___ ___

8. Using accidentals, **RAISE** the following notes a semitone (half step).
   Use the **SAME** letter name. Use whole notes. Name the notes.

10

___ ___ ___ ___ ___

9. Complete the following solid Major triads by adding the third note and the fifth note above each of the given Tonic notes. Use whole notes.

10

Major Triad: F   C   G   F   C   F

10. Match each musical term with the English definition. (Not all definitions will be used.)

Term		Definition
whole tone (whole step)	_____	a) lowest note of a root position triad
semitone (half step)	_____	b) curved line used to show a semitone
penta	_____	c) triad written one note above the other
Major triad	_____	d) five
pentascale	_____	e) three note chord: root, third, fifth
root	_____	f) triad written one note beside the other
Tonic	_____	g) equals two semitones (two half steps)
solid triad	_____	h) stepping down
broken triad	_____	i) pattern of five notes in alphabetical order
semitone slur	_____	j) first degree (note) of a pentascale
		k) shortest distance between two neighbouring keys on the keyboard

10

Lesson 9   Intervals - Harmonic and Melodic

An **INTERVAL** is the distance in pitch between two notes. To identify the **interval number**:

Count each line and each space from the lower note to the higher note.   **OR**   Count each letter name from the lower note to the higher note.

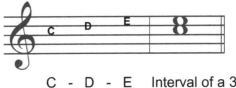

space, line, space   Interval of a 3rd
1   2   3

C - D - E   Interval of a 3rd
1   2   3

♫ **Note:** The name of an interval is written as a number. Example: a first is written as the number 1, a second as the number 2, a third as the number 3, etc.

An **interval of a 1st** is a same line or a same space. It is written as **TWO** notes beside each other on the same line or in the same space. It is also called **UNISON**.

An **interval of a 2nd** is a step. It is always written one note **BESIDE** the next, space to line or line to space. The lowest note of the 2nd is written on the left, with the higher note written on the right.

♫ **Note:** An **interval of a 2nd** is never written with both notes on top of each other.

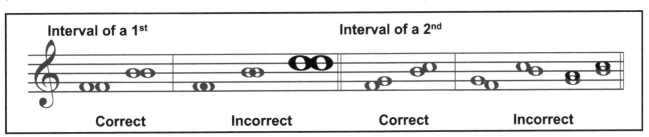

Interval of a 1st		Interval of a 2nd	
Correct	Incorrect	Correct	Incorrect

♫ **Note:** When writing an interval of a 1st on Middle C, one ledger line will be used when both notes are written beside each other. Example:

An **interval of a 3rd** is a skip. It is written from a space to a space skipping a line or from a line to a line skipping a space.

1. Copy the intervals of a 3rd.

2. Write the following intervals **ABOVE** the given notes.

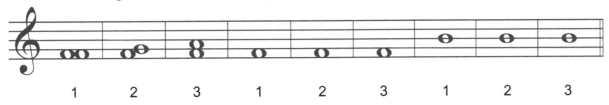

1   2   3   1   2   3   1   2   3

INTERVALS ABOVE a GIVEN NOTE

Intervals can be written **ABOVE a GIVEN NOTE** (getting higher in pitch).

Intervals above C: C - D is a 2ⁿᵈ (C - D: Line - Space).

C - E is a 3ʳᵈ (C - D - E: Line - Space - Line)

Interval: 1   2   3   4   5   6   7   8

1. Name each of the following intervals.

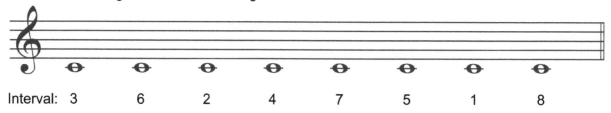

Interval:____   _____   _____   _____   _____   _____   _____   _____

2. Write the following intervals above the given notes. Use whole notes.

Interval: 3   6   2   4   7   5   1   8

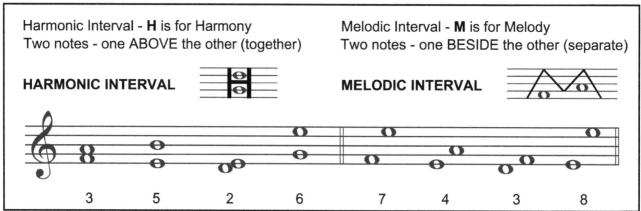

Harmonic Interval - **H** is for Harmony
Two notes - one ABOVE the other (together)

Melodic Interval - **M** is for Melody
Two notes - one BESIDE the other (separate)

HARMONIC INTERVAL   **MELODIC INTERVAL**

3   5   2   6   7   4   3   8

♫ **Note:** Harmonic intervals are played together; melodic intervals are played separately.

3. Write the following intervals above the given notes. (Harmonic - above; Melodic - beside)

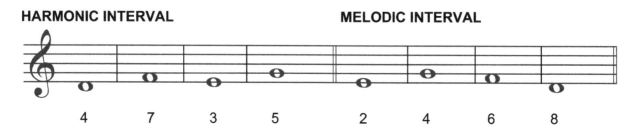

HARMONIC INTERVAL   **MELODIC INTERVAL**

4   7   3   5   2   4   6   8

NAMING HARMONIC and MELODIC INTERVALS

An **INTERVAL** of **1**, **3**, **5** or **7** is always written
with **BOTH** notes in **SPACES** (a space to a space)
or **BOTH** notes on **LINES** (a line to a line).

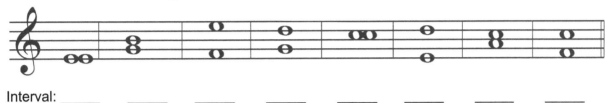

1. Name each of the following harmonic intervals.

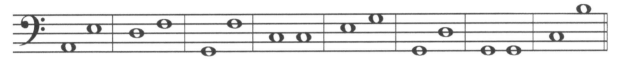

Interval: _____ _____ _____ _____ _____ _____ _____ _____

2. Name each of the following melodic intervals.

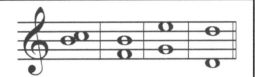

Interval: _____ _____ _____ _____ _____ _____ _____ _____

An **INTERVAL** of **2**, **4**, **6** or **8** is always written
with a note on a **LINE** going to a note in a **SPACE**
or a note in a **SPACE** going to a note on a **LINE**.

3. Name each of the following harmonic intervals.

Interval: _____ _____ _____ _____ _____ _____ _____ _____

4. Name each of the following melodic intervals.

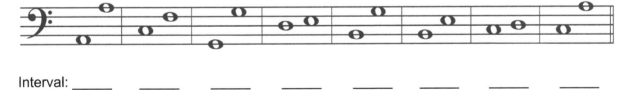

Interval: _____ _____ _____ _____ _____ _____ _____ _____

5. Label each of the following as **H** for harmonic interval or **M** for melodic interval.

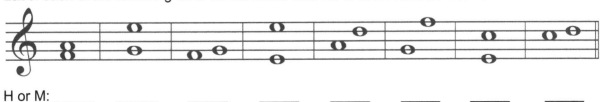

H or M: _____ _____ _____ _____ _____ _____ _____ _____

WRITING HARMONIC and MELODIC INTERVALS

Intervals can be written as **HARMONIC** intervals or as **MELODIC** intervals.

When writing a HARMONIC interval, the "H" means Harmony. Notes are written together, one note ABOVE the other.

♫ **Note:** A 1st and a 2nd are written directly beside (touching) the first note.

1. Write the following harmonic intervals above the given notes.

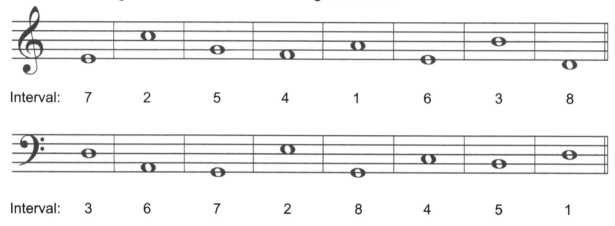

Interval: 7   2   5   4   1   6   3   8

Interval: 3   6   7   2   8   4   5   1

When writing a MELODIC interval, the "M" means Melody. Notes are written separately, one note BESIDE the other.

♫ **Note:** After the 1st note of the melodic interval, leave a small space before writing the 2nd note.

2. Write the following melodic intervals above (and beside) the given notes. Use whole notes.

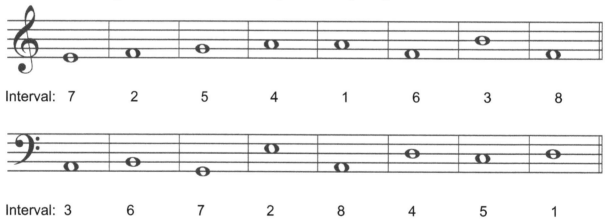

Interval: 7   2   5   4   1   6   3   8

Interval: 3   6   7   2   8   4   5   1

3. Label each of the following as **H** for harmonic interval or **M** for melodic interval.

H or M: _____   _____   _____   _____   _____   _____   _____

TEMPO

Tempo refers to the rate of speed; how fast or slow the music is played.

TEMPO MARKS are terms used in music to indicate different levels of speed.

Term	Definition
largo	very slow and broad, a slow and solemn tempo
adagio	fairly slow, slower than *andante* but not as slow as *largo*
lento	slow
andante	moderately slow, at a moderate walking pace
moderato	at a moderate tempo
allegretto	fairly fast; not as fast as *allegro*
allegro	fast
presto	very fast
prestissimo	as fast as possible

1. Write the term above each tempo definition.

_____	_____	_____
very slow	fairly slow	slow

_____	_____	_____
moderate walking pace	moderate tempo	fairly fast

_____	_____	_____
fast	very fast	as fast as possible

♫ **Note:** The terms used in music are usually Italian words.

Tempo markings are written on the TOP left of the music, above the Time Signature.

2. Copy the music below. Add the tempo markings.

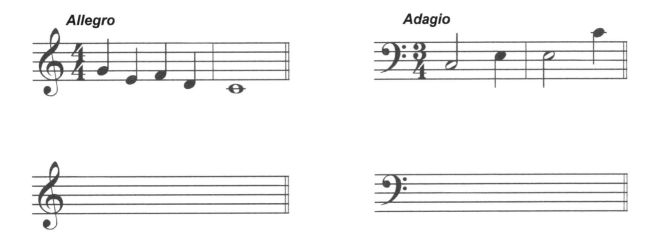

Lesson 9   Review Test

Total Score: ____
100

1. Draw a **Treble Clef** on the staff below. Name the notes in the Treble Clef.

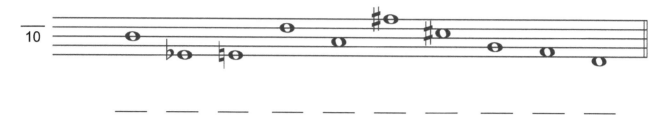

2. Draw a **Bass Clef** on the staff below. Write the following notes in the Bass Clef.
Use **DOTTED HALF** notes.

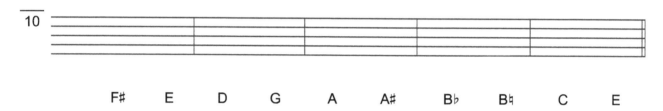

F#   E   D   G   A   A#   B♭   B♮   C   E

3. Scoop each beat. Write the pulse below each Basic Beat. Add **RESTS** below each bracket to complete the measure. Cross off the Basic Beat as each beat is completed.

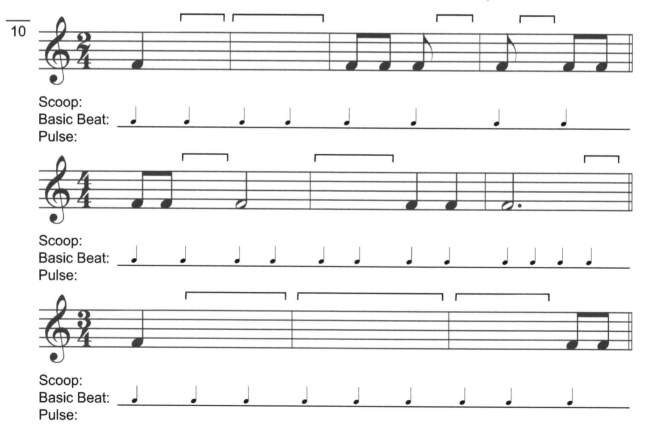

4. Write the following melodic intervals above the given notes. Use whole notes.

10

Intervals: 3   6   1   2   5   4   7   3   8   5

5. a) Write the following Major pentascales, ascending and descending, using accidentals when necessary. Use whole notes.

b) Use Roman Numerals to label the Tonic (**I**) and the Dominant (**V**) notes.

10 c) Write the solid Major Tonic triad. (All lines or all spaces.) Use whole notes. Name the triad.

a) G Major pentascale

b) _____   _____   _____ c) _____ Major triad

a) F Major pentascale

b) _____   _____   _____ c) _____ Major triad

a) C Major pentascale

b) _____   _____   _____ c) _____ Major triad

6. Name the notes. Circle whole tone (whole step) or semitone (half step) for each of the following.

10

_____ _____   _____ _____   _____ _____   _____ _____   _____ _____

whole tone   whole tone   whole tone   whole tone   whole tone

semitone   semitone   semitone   semitone   semitone

7. Using accidentals, **LOWER** the following notes a semitone (half step). Use the **SAME** letter name. Use half notes. Name the notes.

10

_____ _____ _____ _____ _____

8. Using accidentals, **RAISE** the following notes a semitone (half step). Use the **SAME** letter name. Use quarter notes. Name the notes.

10

_____ _____ _____ _____ _____

9. Complete the following solid Major triads by adding the third note and the fifth note above each of the given Tonic notes. Use whole notes.

10

Major Triad: G   C   F   G   C   F

10. Match each musical term with the English definition. (Not all definitions will be used.)

___
10

Term		Definition
harmonic intervals	_____	a) very slow
melodic intervals	_____	b) at a moderate tempo
prestissimo	_____	c) at a walking pace
allegro	_____	d) distance in pitch between 2 notes played separately
presto	_____	e) rate of speed: how fast or slow the music is played
moderato	_____	f) very fast
andante	_____	g) distance in pitch between 2 notes played together
adagio	_____	h) as fast as possible
largo	_____	i) fairly slow
tempo	_____	j) fast
		k) very soft

Lesson 10   Relative Minor Pentascales and Triads

Each Major key has a **RELATIVE MINOR** key. The relative minor key is three semitones and 3 letter names below the Major key. Example: **C Major** - relative minor is **a minor**. C - B - A
1 - 2 - 3

♫ **Note:** UPPER case letters are used for Major keys and lower case letters are used for minor keys.

1. Count down three letter names from the Major key to its relative minor key.

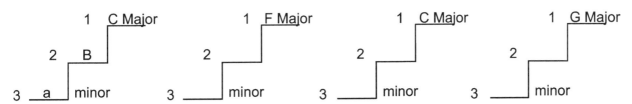

1 C Major   1 F Major   1 C Major   1 G Major
2 B   2   2   2
3 a ⌟ minor   3 ____⌟ minor   3 ____⌟ minor   3 ____⌟ minor

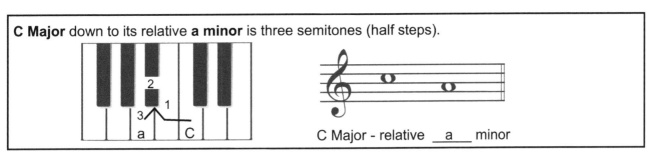

C Major down to its relative **a minor** is three semitones (half steps).

C Major - relative __a__ minor

♫ **Note:** When moving from a Major key DOWN to a minor key, count down three semitones.

2. a) Count down three semitones from the Major key. Name the minor key directly on the keyboard.
    b) Write the minor key note a third below the Major key note. Use whole notes. Name the relative minor key.

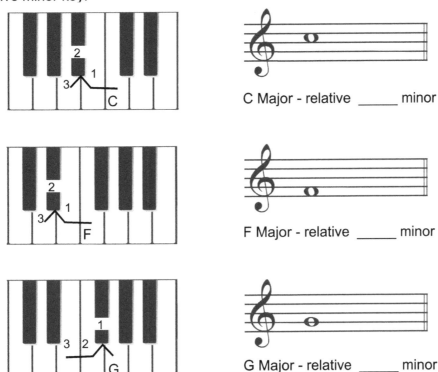

C Major - relative _____ minor

F Major - relative _____ minor

G Major - relative _____ minor

MINOR PENTASCALE - TONIC

A **MINOR PENTASCALE** (penta means 5) is a series of 5 notes or degrees in alphabetical order.

A **caret** sign " ^ " (or hat) above a number ($\hat{3}$) indicates the degree number of the scale.

A minor pentascale uses the following pattern:

$\hat{1}$ |whole tone| $\hat{2}$ semitone $\hat{3}$ |whole tone| $\hat{4}$ |whole tone| $\hat{5}$
　　　　 WT 　　　　 ST 　　　　　 WT 　　　　　 WT

♫ **Note:** In the minor pentascale, the semitone (half step) is always between the 2nd and 3rd degrees.

The first note or degree of a pentascale is called the **TONIC**. The Tonic names the pentascale.

An **upper case** letter is used to name the Tonic note. A **lower case** letter is used to name the minor pentascale. Example: Tonic: **C** This is **c** minor pentascale.

1. a) Copy the following minor pentascales. Use whole notes.
   b) Draw a line from each note on the staff to the corresponding key on the keyboard.
   c) Mark the semitone (half step) with a slur. Name the Tonic. Name the minor pentascale.

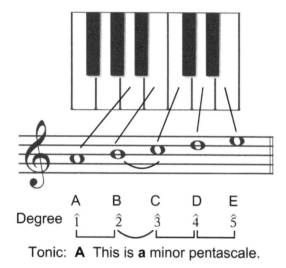

	A	B	C	D	E
Degree	$\hat{1}$	$\hat{2}$	$\hat{3}$	$\hat{4}$	$\hat{5}$

Tonic: **A** This is **a** minor pentascale.

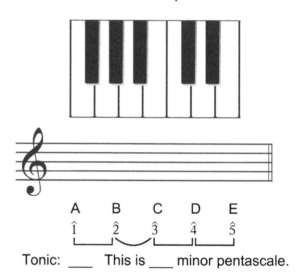

	A	B	C	D	E
Degree	$\hat{1}$	$\hat{2}$	$\hat{3}$	$\hat{4}$	$\hat{5}$

Tonic: ___ This is ___ minor pentascale.

♫ **Note:** An **accidental** may be needed to complete the minor pentascale pattern.

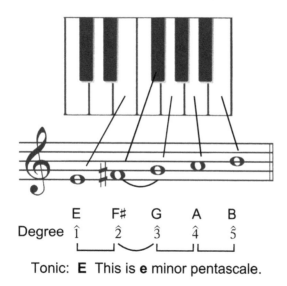

	E	F♯	G	A	B
Degree	$\hat{1}$	$\hat{2}$	$\hat{3}$	$\hat{4}$	$\hat{5}$

Tonic: **E** This is **e** minor pentascale.

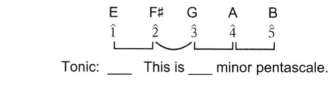

	E	F♯	G	A	B
Degree	$\hat{1}$	$\hat{2}$	$\hat{3}$	$\hat{4}$	$\hat{5}$

Tonic: ___ This is ___ minor pentascale.

MINOR PENTASCALE - TONIC and DOMINANT

In a **MINOR PENTASCALE**, the **TONIC** is the first note and the **DOMINANT** is the fifth note.

1. a) Copy the following minor pentascale.   Use whole notes.
    b) Draw a line from each note on the staff to the corresponding key on the keyboard.
    c) Mark the semitone (half step) with a slur. Name the Tonic (first) and Dominant (fifth) notes.
    d) Name the minor pentascale.

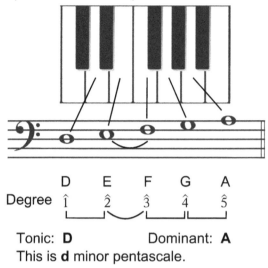
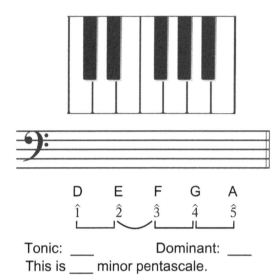

	D	E	F	G	A
Degree	1̂	2̂	3̂	4̂	5̂

Tonic: **D**   Dominant: **A**
This is **d** minor pentascale.

	D	E	F	G	A
Degree	1̂	2̂	3̂	4̂	5̂

Tonic: ___   Dominant: ___
This is ___ minor pentascale.

Roman Numerals are used to identify the Tonic and the Dominant notes. An upper case Roman Numeral is used for the Tonic of the Major pentascale (**I**). A lower case Roman Numeral is used for the Tonic of the minor pentascale (**i**).

♫ **Note:** An upper case Roman Numeral is used for the Dominant (**V**) in both pentascales.

2. a) Following the example: name each note of the minor pentascales below.
    b) Use Roman Numerals to label the Tonic (**i**) and the Dominant (**V**) notes.
    c) Name the minor pentascale.

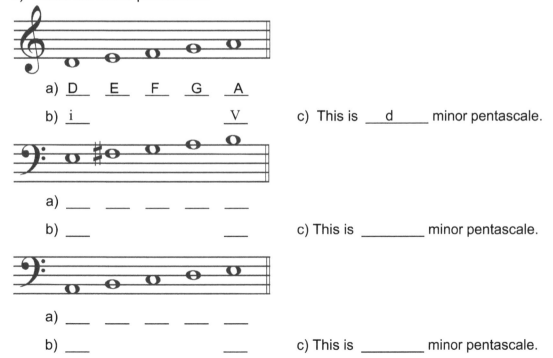

a) D   E   F   G   A
b) i _____ V   c) This is ___d___ minor pentascale.

a) ___ ___ ___ ___ ___
b) ___ ___   c) This is _____ minor pentascale.

a) ___ ___ ___ ___ ___
b) ___ ___   c) This is _____ minor pentascale.

MINOR TONIC TRIAD - TONIC, MEDIANT and DOMINANT

A **MINOR TONIC TRIAD** is a three note chord built on the following degrees of the minor pentascale: Tonic (first) $\hat{1}$, Mediant (third) $\hat{3}$, and Dominant (fifth) $\hat{5}$. ALL LINE notes or ALL SPACE notes.

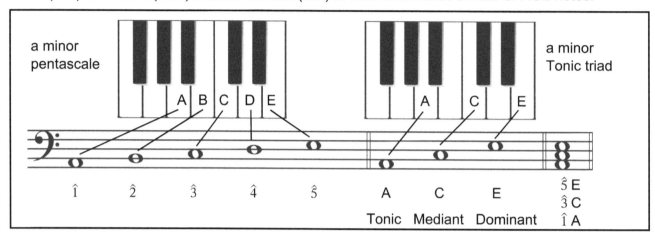

1. Complete the following for e minor and d minor. Use whole notes.
   a) Write the minor pentascale, ascending, in the Bass Clef. Draw a line from each note to the corresponding key on the keyboard. Name the note directly on the keyboard.
   b) Write the Tonic, Mediant and Dominant notes. Name the notes. Draw a line from each note to the corresponding key on the keyboard. Name the notes directly on the keyboard.
   c) Write the 3 notes of the minor Tonic triad. All line notes or all space notes, one above the other.

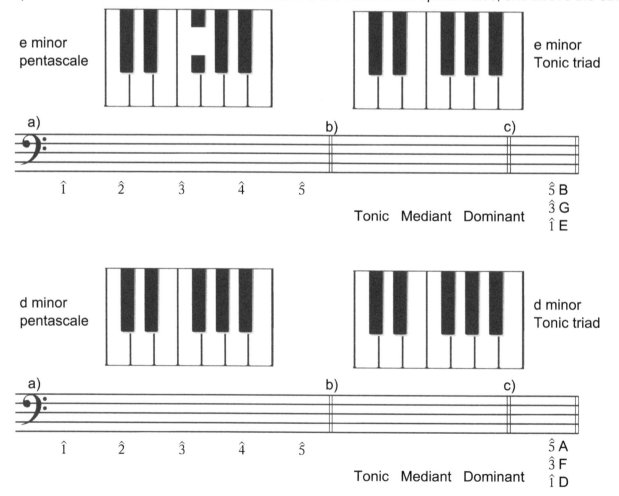

PENTASCALES - ASCENDING and DESCENDING and MINOR TRIADS

PENTASCALES may be written **ASCENDING** and **DESCENDING**. A center bar line is used after the highest note, the Dominant. Roman Numerals are used to label the Tonic (**i**) and the Dominant (**V**).

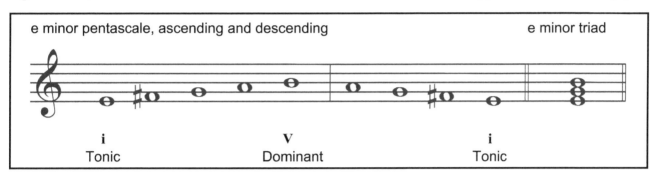

♫ **Note:** If the pentascale contains an accidental, the accidental is repeated after the bar line.

1. a) Write the following minor pentascales, ascending and descending, using accidentals when necessary. Use whole notes.
   b) Use Roman Numerals to label the Tonic (**i**) and the Dominant (**V**) notes.
   c) Write the minor Tonic triad. (All lines or all spaces.) Use whole notes.

a) d minor pentascale

b) _____   _____   _____   c) d minor triad

a) a minor pentascale

b) _____   _____   _____   c) a minor triad

a) e minor pentascale

b) _____   _____   _____   c) e minor triad

SOLID MINOR TRIADS

The lowest note of a **SOLID MINOR TRIAD** in root position (all lines or all spaces) is called the root. The root names the triad.   In the Tonic triad the lowest note is also called the Tonic (first) note.

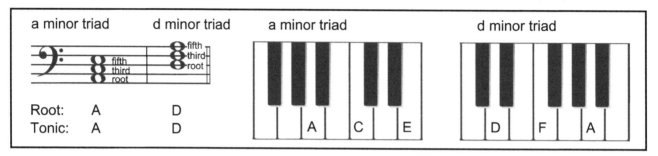

♫ **Note:** A **SOLID** (blocked) triad is written one note **ABOVE** the other.

1. Name the root (lowest note) for each of the following minor triads.

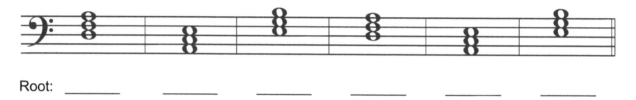

Root: _____   _____   _____   _____   _____   _____

2. Complete the following minor triads by adding the third note and the fifth note above each of the given Tonic notes. Use whole notes. Name the Tonic note.

Tonic: _____   _____   _____   _____   _____   _____

3. Write the note names for each of the following minor triads directly on the keyboard.

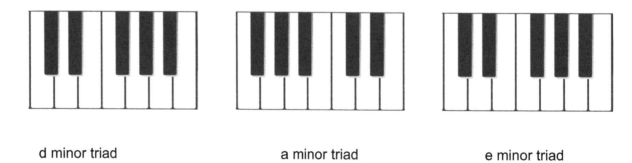

d minor triad   a minor triad   e minor triad

BROKEN MINOR TRIADS

The lowest note of a **BROKEN MINOR TRIAD** in root position (all lines or all spaces) is called the root. The root names the triad. In the Tonic triad the lowest note is also called the Tonic (first) note.

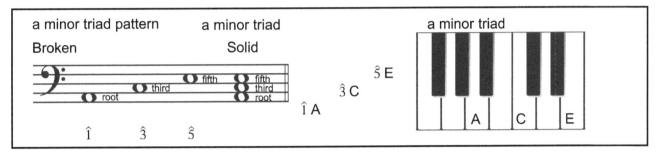

♫ **Note:** A **BROKEN** triad is written one note **BESIDE** the other.

1. a) Name the Tonic note for each of the following minor triads.
   b) Circle Broken or Solid for each of the following minor triads.

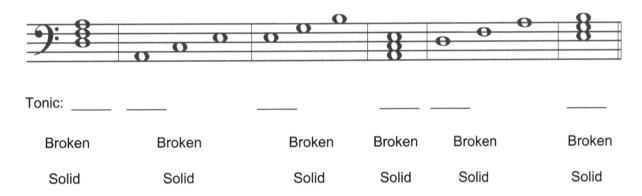

Tonic: _____ _____   _____   _____ _____   _____

Broken	Broken	Broken	Broken	Broken	Broken
Solid	Solid	Solid	Solid	Solid	Solid

♫ **Note:** When the Tonic note is first, the pattern for the broken root position triad is skipping up.

2. Complete the following broken minor triads by adding the third note and the fifth note beside each of the given Tonic notes. Use whole notes. Name each note.

      a minor triad   e minor triad   d minor triad

$\hat{1}$ $\hat{3}$ $\hat{5}$ $\hat{1}$ $\hat{3}$ $\hat{5}$ $\hat{1}$ $\hat{3}$ $\hat{5}$

_____ _____ _____   _____ _____ _____   _____ _____ _____

3. A triad written one note BESIDE the other is called a _____ triad.

4. A triad written one note ABOVE the other is called a _____ triad.

ARTICULATION

Articulation refers to the way that a note can be played. Different types of sound are created by using different articulation (touch). **Articulation marks** are used in music to indicate different sounds.

Term	Definition	Articulation Mark
accent	a stressed note	
fermata	pause, hold for longer than its written value	
staccato	sharply detached	
slur	play notes legato (smoothly)	
tenuto	held, sustained (hold for the full value of the note)	

1. Write the **TERM** above each articulation definition.

a stressed note	pause - hold longer	sharply detached	play notes legato	held, sustained

♫ **Note:** An **ACCENT**, **STACCATO**, **SLUR** and **TENUTO** are all placed close to the notehead and away from the stems. Depending on the stem direction, the articulation is placed above or below the note. A **FERMATA** always goes above the staff.

2. Write the **ARTICULATION MARK** in the appropriate location (either above or below each note).

accent   tenuto   staccato   slur   fermata

3. Copy the music below, adding the articulation markings.

Lesson 10   Review Test

Total Score: ____
100

1. Draw a **Treble Clef** on the staff below. Name the notes.

2. Draw a **Bass Clef** on the staff below. Write the following notes in the Bass Clef.
Use **dotted half** notes.

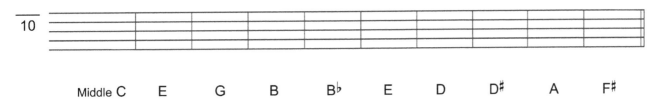

Middle C   E   G   B   B♭   E   D   D♯   A   F♯

3. Write the scoops, Basic Beat and pulse below each measure. Add **RESTS** below each
bracket to complete the measure. Cross off the Basic Beat as each beat is completed.

Scoop:
Basic Beat: _____
Pulse:

Scoop:
Basic Beat: _____
Pulse:

Scoop:
Basic Beat: _____
Pulse:

4. Write the scoops, Basic Beat and pulse below each measure. Add **bar lines**.

10

Scoop:
Basic Beat: _____
Pulse:

5. a) Write the following Major pentascales, ascending and descending, using accidentals when necessary. Use whole notes.
___ b) Use Roman Numerals to label the Tonic (**I**) and the Dominant (**V**) notes.
10 c) Write the solid Major Tonic triad. (All lines or all spaces.) Use whole notes. Name the triad.

a) G Major pentascale

b) _____   _____   _____   c) _____ Major triad

a) F Major pentascale

b) _____   _____   _____   c) _____ Major triad

6. Name the notes. Circle whole tone (whole step) or semitone (half step) for each of the following.

10

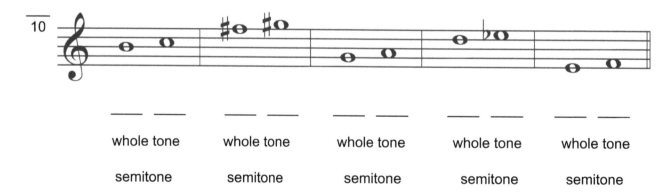

___ ___	___ ___	___ ___	___ ___	___ ___
whole tone	whole tone	whole tone	whole tone	whole tone
semitone	semitone	semitone	semitone	semitone

7. a) Write the following minor pentascales, ascending and descending, using accidentals when necessary. Use whole notes.

___ b) Use Roman Numerals to label the Tonic (**i**) and the Dominant (**V**) notes.

10 c) Write the solid minor Tonic triad. (All lines or all spaces.) Use whole notes. Name the triad.

a) e minor pentascale

b) _____   _____   _____ c) _____ minor triad

a) a minor pentascale

b) _____   _____   _____ c) _____ minor triad

8. a) Draw a **REST** that has the **SAME** value as each note.

b) Name the type of each note/rest (whole, half, quarter or eighth).

10

Note/rest: _____   _____   _____   _____

c) Draw a **NOTE** in space number 1 that has the **SAME** value as each rest.

d) Write the number of beats each rest and each note receives.

Beats: _____   _____   _____   _____   _____   _____   _____   _____

9. Identify the **PATTERN** between each pair of notes in the Bass Clef as:
same line, same space, step up, step down, skip up or skip down. Name the notes.

Notes: _____   _____   _____   _____   _____

Pattern: _____   _____   _____   _____   _____

_____   _____   _____   _____   _____

10. Match each musical term with the English definition. (Not all definitions will be used.)

Term		Definition
minor pentascale	_____	a) refers to the way that a note can be played (touch)
Major pentascale	_____	b) detached
articulation	_____	c) pattern of 5 notes WT WT ST WT
allegro	_____	d) a stressed note
accent	_____	e) three note chord
tenuto	_____	f) pattern of 5 notes WT ST WT WT
staccato	_____	g) at a moderate tempo
fermata	_____	h) held, sustained
moderato	_____	i) fast
slur	_____	j) play the notes legato (smooth)
		k) a pause - hold the note or rest longer than its written value

Lesson 11   Copying Music Correctly

COPYING MUSIC CORRECTLY requires all details to be written exactly as the original.

Minuet
(title)

Moderato
(tempo)

J. S. Bach
(composer)

♫ **Note:** The **title** of the piece often indicates a style, period or musical idea upon which the piece is based. The title of the piece is written at the top center of the music.

1. Name the title of this piece. _____

♫ **Note:** **Composers** are people who write music. Composers express their musical ideas through markings on the music. These markings show the performer how to interpret the music. The composer's name is written at the top right of the music.

2. Name the composer of this piece. _____

♫ **Note:** The **tempo** indicates how fast or slow a piece of music is performed. The tempo is usually indicated by an Italian term. The tempo is written at the top left above the Time Signature.

3. Name and explain the tempo of this piece. _____
_____

♫ **Note:** When copying music, the title, tempo, composer, clef, Time Signature and music notation should be identical to the original.

4. Copy the music in the Bass Clef below.

The Turtle

G. St. Germain

Largo

STACCATOS and SLURS

STACCATOS are dots that are written ABOVE the notehead when the stems go down and BELOW the notehead when the stems go up. A staccato indicates to play the note detached.

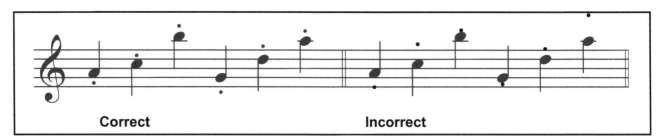

Correct   **Incorrect**

SLURS are curved lines that are written ABOVE the notes when stems go down and BELOW the notes when stems go up. Slurs indicate to play the notes smoothly.

1. Add STACCATO DOTS to all the quarter notes and SLURS to all the groups of eighth notes.

2. Copy the music in the Treble Clef below.

The Rabbit and the Snake

G. St. Germain

DYNAMICS and ARTICULATION

DYNAMICS are signs that indicate the VOLUME at which the music is played. Dynamics add expression to music through various levels of soft to loud sounds.

Dynamic markings are written BELOW the Treble Clef and ABOVE the Bass Clef. When writing music on the Grand Staff dynamics are written between the Treble Clef and the Bass Clef.

ARTICULATION are signs that indicate the TOUCH at which notes may be played. Articulation adds interest to the music by using a variety of different sounds.

Articulation markings (accent, staccato, slur and tenuto) are placed close to the notehead and away from the stems. A fermata is always written above the Treble Clef and above the Bass Clef.

♫ **Note: Copying Music Correctly** requires all details to be written exactly as the original.

1. Copy the music in the Grand Staff below.

The Magician

Review Test

Total Score: ____

100

1.   Draw a **Treble Clef** on the staff below. Name the notes.

10

_____   _____   _____   _____   _____   _____   _____   _____   _____   _____

2.   Draw a **Bass Clef** on the staff below. Write the following notes in the Bass Clef.
      Use **dotted half** notes.

10

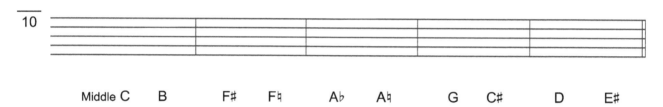

Middle C   B   F#   F♮   A♭   A♮   G   C#   D   E#

3.   Write the scoops, Basic Beat and pulse below each measure. Add **RESTS** below each
      bracket to complete the measure. Cross off the Basic Beat as each beat is completed.

10

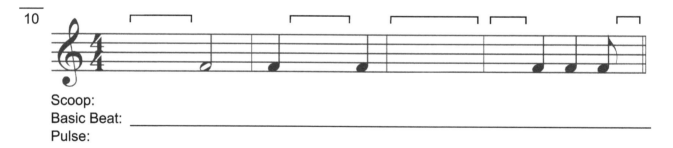

Scoop:
Basic Beat: _____
Pulse:

Scoop:
Basic Beat: _____
Pulse:

4. Write the scoops, Basic Beat and pulse below each measure. Add **bar lines**.

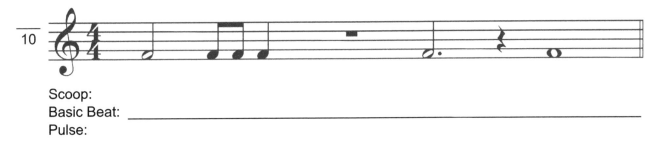

Scoop:
Basic Beat: _____
Pulse:

5. a) Write the following Major pentascales, ascending and descending, using accidentals when necessary. Use whole notes.
   b) Use Roman Numerals to label the Tonic (**I**) and the Dominant (**V**) notes.
   c) Write the solid Major Tonic triad. (All lines or all spaces.) Use whole notes. Name the triad.

a) F Major pentascale

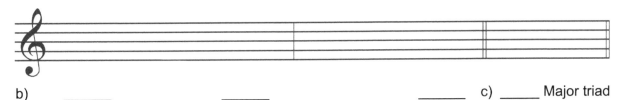

b) _____   _____   _____   c) _____ Major triad

a) C Major pentascale

b) _____   _____   _____   c) _____ Major triad

6. Name the notes. Circle whole tone (whole step) or semitone (half step) for each of the following.

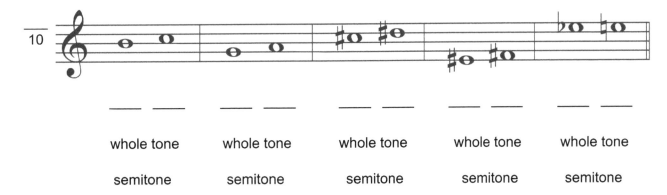

____ ____   ____ ____   ____ ____   ____ ____   ____ ____

whole tone   whole tone   whole tone   whole tone   whole tone

semitone   semitone   semitone   semitone   semitone

7. a) Write the following minor pentascales, ascending and descending, using accidentals when necessary. Use whole notes.

b) Use Roman Numerals to label the Tonic (**i**) and the Dominant (**V**) notes.

___
10 c) Write the solid minor Tonic triad. (All lines or all spaces.) Use whole notes. Name the triad.

a) d minor pentascale

b) _____   _____   _____ c) _____ minor triad

a) e minor pentascale

b) _____   _____   _____ c) _____ minor triad

8. Copy the music in the Treble Clef below.

___
10

Off to School

Andante

G. St. Germain

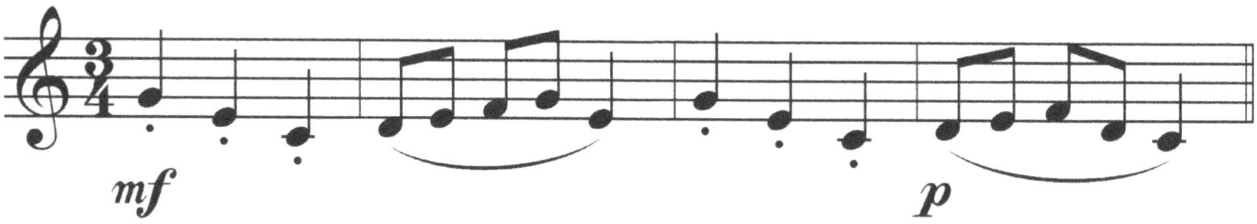

9. Identify the **PATTERN** between each pair of notes in the Bass Clef as:
same line, same space, step up, step down, skip up or skip down. Name the notes.

Notes: _____ ∨↗ _____   _____ ∨↗ _____   _____ ∨↗ _____   _____ ∨↗ _____   _____ ∨↗ _____

Pattern: _____   _____   _____   _____   _____

_____   _____   _____   _____   _____

10. Match each musical term with the English definition. (Not all definitions will be used.)

Term		Definition
semitone (half step)	_____	a) refers to the way that a note can be played (touch)
title	_____	b) slow
sharp	_____	c) pattern of 5 notes WT WT ST WT
lento	_____	d) raises a note one semitone (half step)
Major pentascale	_____	e) indicates levels of soft to loud sounds (volume)
allegretto	_____	f) pattern of 5 notes WT ST WT WT
minor pentascale	_____	g) fairly fast, a little slower than *allegro*
dynamics	_____	h) lowers a note one semitone (half step)
articulation	_____	i) person who writes music
composer	_____	j) name of the piece of music
		k) shortest distance between two neighbouring keys on the keyboard

Lesson 12   Analysis and Musical Terms

ANALYSIS of a musical piece is examining the details of the composition before beginning to learn or perform the piece. Analysis of music provides us with a better understanding of the piece.

1. Analyze the following piece of music by answering the questions below.

Stars at Night

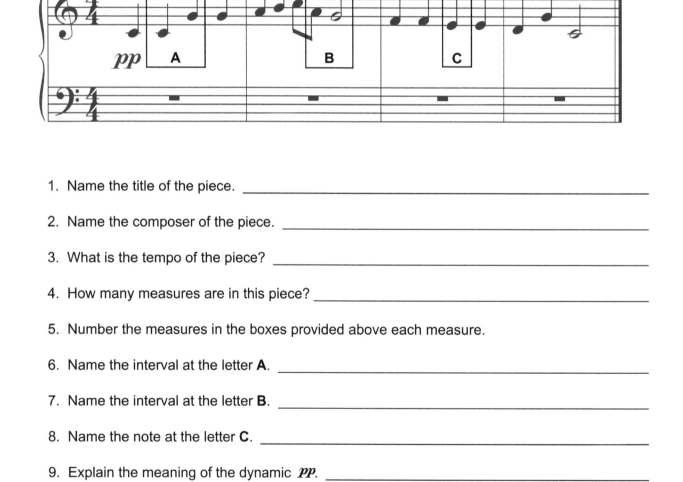

1. Name the title of the piece. _____

2. Name the composer of the piece. _____

3. What is the tempo of the piece? _____

4. How many measures are in this piece? _____

5. Number the measures in the boxes provided above each measure.

6. Name the interval at the letter **A**. _____

7. Name the interval at the letter **B**. _____

8. Name the note at the letter **C**. _____

9. Explain the meaning of the dynamic *pp*. _____

10. Explain the meaning of the sign at the letter **D**. _____

    _____

2. Analyze the following piece of music by answering the questions below.

Minuet

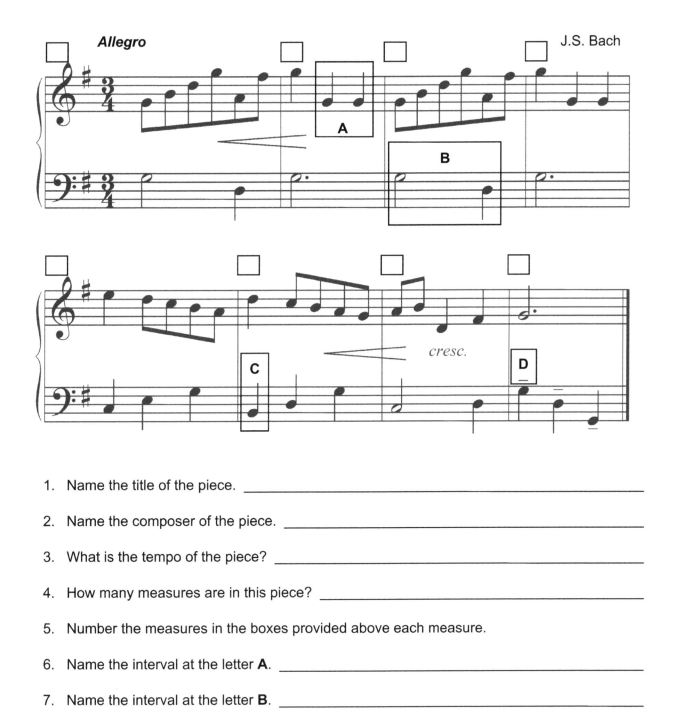

1. Name the title of the piece. _____

2. Name the composer of the piece. _____

3. What is the tempo of the piece? _____

4. How many measures are in this piece? _____

5. Number the measures in the boxes provided above each measure.

6. Name the interval at the letter **A**. _____

7. Name the interval at the letter **B**. _____

8. Name the note at the letter **C**. _____

9. Explain the meaning of *crescendo* (*cresc.*). _____

10. Explain the meaning of the sign at the letter **D**. _____

MUSICAL TERMS and SIGNS

Dynamic Terms	Symbol or Sign	Definition
crescendo	cresc. or ⟨	becoming louder
diminuendo	dim. or ⟩	becoming softer
decrescendo	decresc. or ⟩	becoming softer
fortissimo	_ff_	very loud
forte	_f_	loud
mezzo forte	_mf_	medium loud (moderately loud)
mezzo piano	_mp_	medium soft (moderately soft)
piano	_p_	soft
pianissimo	_pp_	very soft

1. Dynamics are signs that indicate the _____ at which the music is played.

Tempo Terms	Definition
largo	very slow
lento	slow
adagio	fairly slow
andante	at a moderate walking pace, moderately slow
moderato	at a moderate tempo
allegretto	fairly fast; a little slower than _allegro_
allegro	fast
presto	very fast
prestissimo	as fast as possible

2. Tempo terms are signs that indicate the _____ at which the music is played.

Musical Terms	Definition
accidental	sharp, flat or natural sign in front of a note
bar line	divides staff into equal measures
degrees of a scale	$\hat{1}$, $\hat{2}$, $\hat{3}$, $\hat{4}$, $\hat{5}$
flat	lowers a note one semitone (half step)
ledger line	short line used for Middle C
Major pentascale	5 notes in alphabetical order in the pattern of WT WT ST WT
measure	a unit of musical time
minor pentascale	5 notes in alphabetical order in the pattern of WT ST WT WT
natural sign	cancels a sharp or a flat
octave	8 notes beginning and ending with the same letter name
pitch	high or low sounds
sharp	raises a note one semitone (half step)
skip	line note to the next line note or space note to the next space note
step	line note to the next space note or space note to the next line note
Time Signature	indicates how many beats in a measure
triad	3 note chord: Tonic, Mediant and Dominant notes of the scale

3. Accidentals are signs that raise or lower the pitch. Name 3 accidental signs.

_____   _____   _____

Lesson 12   Final Prep 1 Exam

1. Draw a **Treble Clef** on the staff below. Name the notes.

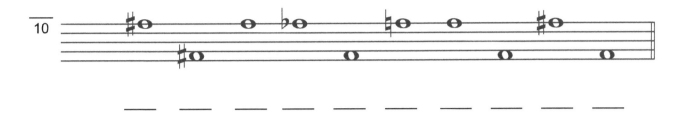

2. Add **STEMS** and a **BEAM** to form a pair of beamed eighth notes in each measure.
Name the notes.

3. Write the scoops, Basic Beat and pulse below each measure. Add **RESTS** below each
bracket to complete the measure. Cross off the Basic Beat as each beat is completed.

Scoop:
Basic Beat: _____
Pulse:

Scoop:
Basic Beat: _____
Pulse:

4. Name the following harmonic intervals.

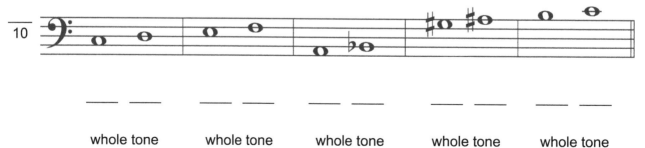

5. a) Write the following pentascales, ascending and descending, using accidentals when necessary. Use whole notes.
   b) Use Roman Numerals to label the Tonic (**I**) and the Dominant (**V**) notes in the Major pentascale, and the Tonic (**i**) and the Dominant (**V**) notes in the minor pentascale.
   c) Write the solid Tonic triad. (All lines or all spaces.) Use whole notes. Name the triad.

10

   a) G Major pentascale

   b) _____   _____   _____   c) _____ Major triad

   a) a minor pentascale

   b) _____   _____   _____   c) _____ minor triad

6. Name the notes. Circle whole tone (whole step) or semitone (half step) for each of the following.

10

whole tone   whole tone   whole tone   whole tone   whole tone

semitone   semitone   semitone   semitone   semitone

7. Copy the music in the Bass Clef below.

8. Identify the **PATTERN** between each pair of notes in the Treble Clef as:
same line, same space, step up, step down, skip up or skip down. Name the notes.

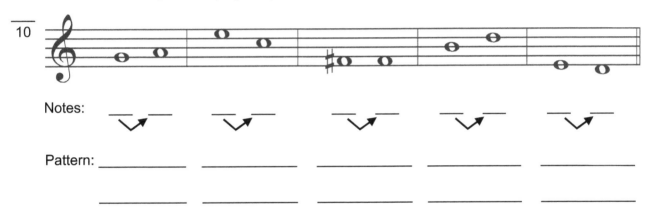

Notes: _____ _____ _____ _____ _____

Pattern: _____ _____ _____ _____ _____

_____ _____ _____ _____ _____

9. Match each musical term with the English definition. (Not all definitions will be used.)

Term		Definition
black keys	_____	a) indicates how many beats in a measure
staff	_____	b) 2 notes played together, both at the same time
patterns	_____	c) sharp, flat or natural sign in front of a note
harmonic interval	_____	d) equal to two semitones (half steps)
Time Signature	_____	e) group of 2 and group of 3 keys
pulse	_____	f) 2 notes played separately, one after the other
accidentals	_____	g) 3 note chord (Tonic, Mediant and Dominant)
whole tone (whole step)	_____	h) music moving from one note to the next note
melodic interval	_____	i) where the rhythmic emphasis falls in a measure
triad	_____	j) five lines and four spaces
		k) shortest distance between two neighbouring keys on the keyboard

10. Analyze the following piece of music by answering the questions below.

German Dance

F. J. Haydn

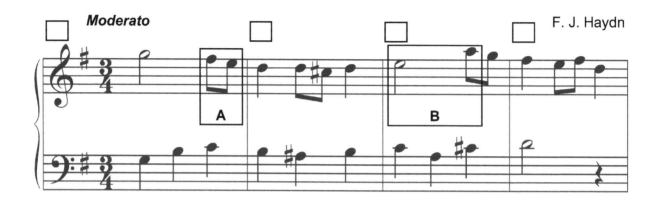

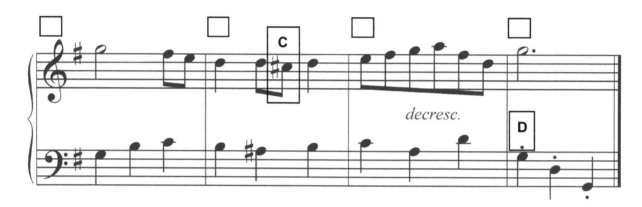

a) Name the title of the piece. _____

b) Name the composer of the piece. _____

c) What is the tempo of the piece? _____

d) How many measures are in this piece? _____

e) Number the measures in the boxes provided above each measure.

f) Name the interval at the letter **A**. _____

g) Name the interval at the letter **B**. _____

h) Name the note at the letter **C**. _____

i) Explain the meaning of *decrescendo* (*decresc.*). _____

j) Explain the meaning of the sign at the letter **D**. _____

UltimateMusicTheory.com

ULTIMATE
MUSIC THEORY

The Ultimate Music Theory™ Program and Supplemental Workbooks help students prepare for nationally recognized theory examinations including the Royal Conservatory of Music.

UMT Workbooks plus UMT Supplemental Workbooks = RCM Theory Levels

Prep 1 Music Theory Workbook plus:

♪ PREP LEVEL Supplemental　=　Preparatory Theory (No Exam)

♪ LEVEL 1 Supplemental　　　=　Level 1 Theory (No Exam)

Prep 2 Music Theory Workbook plus:

♪ LEVEL 2 Supplemental　　　=　Level 2 Theory (No Exam)

♪ LEVEL 3 Supplemental　　　=　Level 3 Theory (No Exam)

Basic Music Theory Workbook plus:

♪ LEVEL 4 Supplemental　　　=　Level 4 Theory (No Exam)

♪ LEVEL 5 Supplemental　　　=　Level 5 Theory (Exam - 1 hour)

Intermediate Music Theory Workbook plus:

♪ LEVEL 6 Supplemental　　　=　Level 6 Theory (Exam - 2 hours)

♪ LEVEL 7 Supplemental　　　=　Level 7 Theory (Exam - 2 hours)

Advanced Music Theory Workbook plus:

♪ LEVEL 8 Supplemental　　　=　Level 8 Theory (Exam - 2 hours)

Complete Music Theory Workbook plus:

♪ COMPLETE Supplemental　　=　Level 8 Theory (Exam - 2 hours)

UltimateMusicTheory.com

ULTIMATE MUSIC THEORY GUIDE - PREP 1

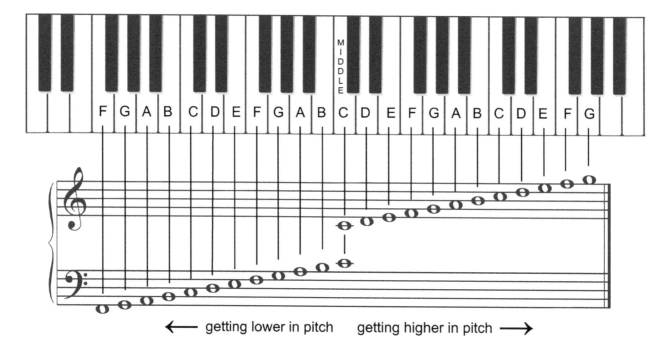

← getting lower in pitch   getting higher in pitch →

An **ACCIDENTAL** is a sign that raises or lowers the pitch one semitone (half step).

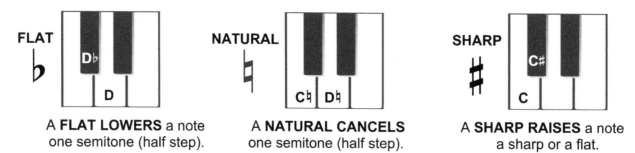

FLAT

A **FLAT LOWERS** a note one semitone (half step).

NATURAL

A **NATURAL CANCELS** one semitone (half step).

SHARP

A **SHARP RAISES** a note a sharp or a flat.

An **INTERVAL** is the distance in pitch between two notes.

HARMONIC Interval - **H** is for Harmony
Two notes - one ABOVE the other (together)

MELODIC Interval - **M** is for Melody
Two notes - one BESIDE the other (separate)

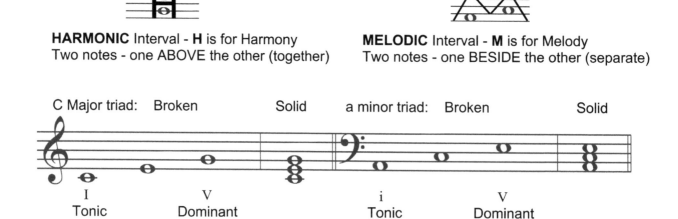

C Major triad: Broken   Solid   a minor triad: Broken   Solid

I   V   i   V
Tonic   Dominant   Tonic   Dominant

UltimateMusicTheory.com

ULTIMATE MUSIC THEORY CHART - PREP 1

Major to relative minor

C Major pentascale
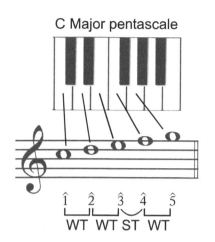

$\hat{1}$ $\hat{2}$ $\hat{3}$ $\hat{4}$ $\hat{5}$

WT WT ST WT

Down 3 semitones (half steps)

1   2   3

C   B   A

Down 3 letter names

C Major - relative a minor

a minor pentascale
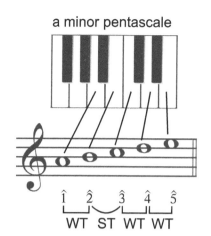

$\hat{1}$ $\hat{2}$ $\hat{3}$ $\hat{4}$ $\hat{5}$

WT ST WT WT

Time Signature   Bar Line   Double Bar Line   Final Bar Line

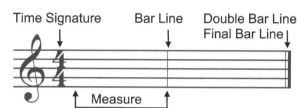

Measure

Time Signature

Top Number: Pulse
Strong + weak; Medium + weak
weak ~ weak; weak ~ Medium

Bottom Number: ♩ = one beat
Basic Beat is one quarter note

PATTERNS

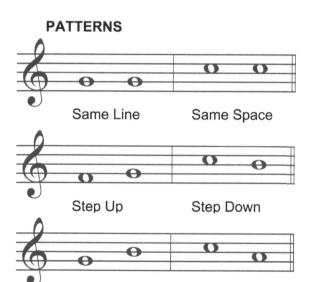

Same Line   Same Space

Step Up   Step Down

Skip Up   Skip Down

TIME SIGNATURES

2/4   S   w

3/4   S   w   w

4/4   S   w   M   w
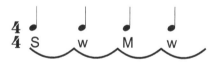

Whole	**Dotted Half**	**Half**	**Quarter**	**Eighth**	**Two Eighth**
note/rest	note	note/rest	note/rest	note/rest	notes
4 beats	3 beats	2 beats	1 beat	½ beat	1 beat